# Reflections on Growing Up Disabled

Edited by **Reginald L. Jones**

College of Human and Rural Development

University of Alaska, Fairbanks, AK 99701
**A product of the ERIC Clearinghouse on Handicapped and Gifted Children**

The Council for Exceptional Children

**Library of Congress Cataloging in Publication Data**
Main entry under title:

Reflections on growing up disabled.

    Bibliography: p.
    1. Handicapped children—Addresses, essays, lectures.
2. Handicapped children—Biography—Addresses, essays,
lectures. I. Jones, Reginald L. II. ERIC Clearinghouse on
Handicapped and Gifted Children.
HV888.R43 1983    362.4'092'2 [B]    82-19823
ISBN 0-86586-134-X

A product of the ERIC Clearinghouse on Handicapped and Gifted
Children.

Published in 1983 by The Council for Exceptional Children, 1920
Association Drive, Reston, Virginia 22091-1589

Development of this publication was supported by the National
Support Systems Project, under a grant from the Division of
Personnel Preparation, Bureau of Education for the Handicapped.
US Office of Education, Department of Health, Education, and
Welfare. The points of view expressed in this publication are
those of the authors and do not necessarily reflect the positions of
the US Office of Education, and no official endorsement by the
US Office of Education should be inferred.

The material in this publication was prepared pursuant to
contract no. 400-81-0031 with the National Institute of Education,
U.S. Department of Education. Contractors undertaking such
projects under Government sponsorship are encouraged to
express freely their judgment in professional and technical
matters. Prior to publication, the manuscript was critically
reviewed for determination of professional quality. Points of view
or opinions, however, do not necessarily represent the official
view or opinions of either the clearinghouse's parent organization
or the National Institute of Education.

# Contents

## The Council for Exceptional Children

Founded in 1922, The Council for Exceptional Children (CEC) is a professional association committed to advancing the education of exceptional children and youth, both gifted and handicapped.

CEC, with 50,000 members, supports every child's right to an appropriate education and seeks to influence local, state, and federal legislation relating to handicapped and gifted children. CEC conducts conventions and conferences and maintains an information center with computer search services and an outstanding collection of special education literature.

In addition to its membership periodicals, *Exceptional Children* and *TEACHING Exceptional Children*, CEC has a publications list of 75 titles including monographs, texts, workshop kits, films, and filmstrips.

Council Headquarters are at 1920 Association Drive, Reston, Virginia 22091.


## The ERIC Clearinghouse on Handicapped and Gifted Children

The ERIC Clearinghouse on Handicapped and Gifted Children (ERIC-EC) is one of 16 clearinghouses in a national information system funded by the National Institute of Education, U.S. Department of Education. Since 1966, ERIC-EC has been housed with The Council for Exceptional Children.

ERIC-EC collects, abstracts, and indexes special education documents and journals for the central ERIC database as well as for its own computer file and publications. Other activities include computer searches, search reprints, and publications. Address inquiries to the ERIC Clearinghouse at 1920 Association Drive, Reston, Virginia 22091.

# Contributors

**Dixie Branner Baker,** at the time of writing, was Assistant Director of State Education Agency Relations, National Information Center for Special Education Materials, University of Southern California, Los Angeles.

**Dale Brown** is Public Information Specialist, President's Committee on Employment of the Handicapped, and founder, National Network of Learning Disabled Adults.

**Zannet Coleman** is Instructional Counselor, California School for the Deaf at Fremont.

**Dorothy DeSimone** is a retired rehabilitation counselor and paralegal advocate, Center for Independent Living, Berkeley, California.

**Barbara B. Galtelli** is Special Education Supervisor, Crittenden County Special Education Cooperative, Marion, Arkansas.

**Bobby G. Greer** is Professor, Department of Special Education and Rehabilitation, Memphis State University, Tennessee.

**Stephen Hofmann,** at the time of writing, was educational consultant to parents of disabled children, Berkeley, California.

**Leo M. Jacobs** is a retired coordinator of continuing and community education for the deaf in the San Francisco Bay Metropolitan area and instructor at the California School for the Deaf at Berkeley.

**Kenneth Jernigan** is Executive Director, American Brotherhood for the Blind, and Director, National Center for the Blind, Baltimore, Maryland.

**Reginald L. Jones** is Professor, Department of Afro-American Studies, University of California, Berkeley

**Diane Lattin** is a retired member of the President's Committee on Employment of the Handicapped, and editor, *Disabled, USA.*

The late **Kathryn A. (Gorham) Morton** was Director, Family and Community Services, Montgomery County, Maryland, Association for Retarded Citizens, Inc.

**John Umbreit** is Professor, Department of Special Education, College of Education, University of Arizona, Tucson.

**Michael Winter** is Executive Director, Center for Independent Living, Inc., Berkeley, California.

# Foreword

An argument once occurred over how to implement the United States' "Good Neighbor" policy toward Latin America. Should we send to our southern neighbors people with correct attitudes who can articulate our intentions? Or would it be better to have emissaries who know how to dig wells, improve agriculture, and control infectious diseases? Would it be better to express neighborliness through attitudes or practical means? The answer, probably, is both; that is, we should be aware of our attitudes and able to articulate them and at the same time, we should be able to express them directly in all forms of behavior.

An attitude is a general predisposition that characterizes the way we approach or avoid situations or people. Attitudes can be problems or important assets; they can be helpful or hurtful; they can be rigid or changeable. Often, when a major change takes place in social policy, people's attitudes must be changed or the policy cannot succeed.

In 1975, the year Public Law 94-142 (the 1975 Education for All Handicapped Children Act) was passed by the U.S. Congress, Dr. Edwin W. Martin, then Deputy Commissioner of Education and Director of the Bureau of Education for the Handicapped in the U.S. Office of Education, stressed the importance of attitudes toward handicapped persons in the implementation of the law. He said

> We must recognize that helping teachers to deal with the uniqueness of children is basically an attitudinal problem. It is a problem that touches the belief systems and self-concepts of teachers.

If educators are to realize the high principles expressed in Public Law 94-142, we must become informed about attitudes: how they are defined, how they are formed and measured, how they can be changed, and how they are perceived by handicapped individuals.

In this volume, Dr. Jones has brought together the expressions of persons who are very much on the scene in special education and related areas. Here are the voices of handicapped persons, their parents, and their close associates talking about the attitudes which they experience from the people who touch their lives.

I am grateful to Dr. Jones for his efforts in bringing all these views together and for his continuing interest and assistance in the activities of the National Support Systems Project.

*Maynard C. Reynolds*
*Director, National Support*
*Systems Project*

# Preface

Too often, special education and rehabilitation attitude literature lacks contributions from disabled persons. Thus we have studies of attitudes toward deaf, blind, or learning disabled persons, for example, but all too rarely are persons in these disability groups given the opportunity to express their own views—on attitudinal or on other matters intimately affecting their lives. The present volume is designed to fill a real void in the attitudinal literature by presenting firsthand accounts of the experiences and perceptions of disabled persons themselves, as well as the views of parents of disabled children.

The volume covers the full developmental continuum: childhood (Umbreit and Baker), adolescence (Winters and De Simone), and adulthood (Lattin, Hofmann, Brown, Jacobs, Coleman, and Jernigan). Unfortunately, young children are not able to write a chapter for themselves. Thus, Umbreit and Baker were asked to survey the literature on children, including anecdotal accounts of disabled adults' childhood experiences. Winter and De Simone draw more directly on their own experiences and those of disabled adolescents in a "rap group" to present a portrait of the attitudinal perceptions and barriers faced by such adolescents. They give special attention to the exacerbating effects of disability on the typically difficult adolescent period and they indicate how parents, school personnel, and other important adults can facilitate or impede the adjustment of disabled adolescents.

Six chapters present the different perspectives of disabled adults. Lattin recounts her experiences in school and work and indicates how they influenced her attitudes toward self and education. She strongly emphasizes the value of education in mainstream settings, a point also emphasized by Hofmann. Hofmann, however, analyzes barries that hamper interaction between handicapped and nonhandicapped persons and indicates what must be done to overcome these barriers.

Brown, writing from the perspective of a learning disabled adult, graphically describes her determination to overcome her nameless handicap in school, home, and college and recounts the dramatic discovery of the nature of her disability; she concludes her chapter by identifying the interpersonal encounters that facilitated or impeded her adjustment.

Chapters by Jacobs, Jernigan, and Coleman address the attitudes they experienced as deaf and blind persons. If the papers are somewhat strident in tone it is to emphasize the discrimination which deaf and blind persons encounter and the measures that must be taken to curtail it. Jacobs stresses the notion that hearing people must accept the manual mode of conversation and that deaf people must communicate in a manner that fosters interpersonal adjustment; the latter, in large measure, means developing relationships with other deaf people. Coleman writes from the perspective of a Black adult who is also deaf. Jernigan focuses upon society's misconceptions and stereotypes of blindness, which are barriers to the integration of blind persons into the community. He reminds us that the position of blind people on matters of integration is one of assertiveness and insistence upon full participation in society.

Although the views of Jacobs and Jernigan are shared by a majority of deaf and blind persons, there are, of course, other ways of looking at the matters under discussion. We have good reason to believe that all views expressed by the authors represent mainstream thinking, but it must be noted that each author was asked only to present his or her own experiences and perceptions.

The two final papers treat the attitudes and experiences of parents of disabled children. The late Kathryn Morton discussed her experiences as a parent of a handicapped child; she noted changes in attitude over the years, possible barriers to attitudinal change among parents, and what must be done, especially by parents and school people, to effect attitude change. Greer and Galtelli are also parents of disabled children; they argue convincingly for an analysis of the irrational assumptions (attitudes) held both by parents of disabled children and by the professionals who serve them.

I am immensely indebted to the contributors who shared their feelings and experiences with us and who critiqued and responded to one another's papers and to the concept of the volume. I am also indebted to a small group of colleagues who brought their considerable expertise to bear on the volume, from conception to final chapter drafts: Dr. Oris Amos, Wright State University; Dr. Samuel Guskin, Indiana University; and Dr. Maynard Reynolds. It is unlikely that the volume could have come to fruition without the support of Dr. Reynolds, Director of the National Support Systems Project, University of Minnesota, whose organization sponsored and supported preparation of the manuscript. Dr. Reynolds and his staff, especially Karen Lundholm and Sylvia Rosen, helped to remove many barriers to a timely completion of this work.

I am indebted to Ms. Margaret Brewton and Ms. Norma Coleman who ably assisted in preparation of the manuscript. Finally, I express sincere appreciation to Dr. June Jordan, Editor in Chief of CEC publications, who provided wise counsel in conceptualizing and structuring the volume, and to her staff in readying the work for publication.

*Reginald L. Jones*
*University of California, Berkeley*

# CHAPTER ONE

# Reflections of Disabled Children

## John Umbreit
## Dixie Branner Baker

A disability's full effect on a child is likely to extend far beyond the immediate physical and/or mental limitations. Whether as a direct result of frustrations emanating from the disability itself or as a function of socialization, the disabled child's self-concept is bound to be affected. In this first brief chapter, personal accounts serve to highlight the major events that authors in later chapters will deal with more fully. The accounts reported offer unique and revealing insights into the characters and personalities of their authors. It must be remembered, however, that they are highly individual and generally written in retrospect by highly motivated, talented, successful, and truly "exceptional" disabled persons. Thus the reader is cautioned to view the accounts as unique case studies that offer glimpses into the personal experiences of their authors and not as reference points for making generalizations.

The personal accounts cited in this chapter cover four disabilities: Carlson and French describe the effects of being physically handicapped; Dickinson speaks as a person who is visually handicapped; Keller presents an eloquent account of her experiences as a deaf and blind person; and Parker describes the effects of epilepsy on her life. Their personal accounts reflect the following:

...early lack of awareness:

I sometimes wondered why I was an object of pity; I had no idea

---

*Note*: This chapter is excerpted from "Self-Perceptions of Disabled Children" by J. Umbreit and D. B. Baker.

that I was abnormal—it was all natural enough since I was "born that way." (Carlson, 1941, p. 7)

No child is born with an awareness that he (or she) is blind. I was not. I knew and played with other children my own age who, I suppose, knew that I was blind. (Dickinson, 1975, p. 249)

. . .beginnings of realization of a "difference":

The realization that I was not quite like everyone else came gradually and was not fully absorbed until I was, perhaps, about thirteen. (Dickinson, 1975, p. 249)

As I approached adolescence, I became so self-conscious about my handicaps and so introspective that I must have impressed my teachers as being mentally retarded. For the first time the realization that I was different from other people sank home. When I saw that none of my schoolmates were afflicted as I was, I began to wonder if there were some hereditary curse upon me. I fell into the habit of brooding upon my handicaps, and these seemed to grow steadily worse. (Carlson, 1941, p. 22)

My studies provided a vicarious new atmosphere where I could live, escaping the harshness of my physical reality . . . What I remember most about this period were my feelings of uselessness and the resultant depressions. (French, 1975, p. 240)

I do not remember when I first realized that I was different from other people; but I knew it before my teacher came to me. I had noticed that my mother and my friends did not use signs as I did when they wanted anything done, but talked with their mouths. (Keller, 1961, p. 24)

. . .resultant frustrations:

Sometimes I stood between two persons who were conversing and touched their lips. I could not understand, and was vexed. I moved my lips and gesticulated frantically without result. This made me so angry at times that I kicked and screamed until I was exhausted . . . the desire to express myself grew. The few signs I used became less and less adequate, and my failures to make myself understood were invariably followed by outbursts of passion. I felt as if invisible hands were holding me, and I made frantic efforts to free myself. I struggled—not that struggling helped matters, but the spirit of resistance was strong within me; I generally broke down in tears and physical exhaustion. If my mother happened to be near I crept into her arms, too miserable even to remember the cause of the tempest. After awhile the need of some means of communication became so urgent that these out-bursts occurred daily, sometimes hourly. (Keller, 1961, pp. 24, 29–30)

...denials and searching for cures:

In the prayer meetings that I attended as a child, the ceremony of laying hands on the afflicted was observed and often the congre-gation would be overjoyed by the miraculous effect this had on me. But the cure was never permanent ... (But) my mother never gave up hope of my cure ... she took me from one clinic to another ... sometimes she rebelled against (the) verdict and tried all manner of quack medicines and healing cults ... Time after time my hopes were raised high and then brought crashing down. (Carlson, 1941, pp. 15–17)

...pressures at school:

Well-meaning teachers became anxious and over-solicitous, which called attention to my problem and gave dependence free rein. Some of my classmates resented this, and sensed the favoritism toward me. This made it hard for me to make friends ... I began to feel different from other girls. I could not stand criticism. It was one thing to feel that I was different because I was an epi-leptic but, in addition, the feeling that I was not capable of keep-ing up with the other girls made me feel inadequate as well ... Through those years from the first grade to the fifth grade I be-came very, very sensitive. I was extremely insecure. I knew that *I was different!* (Parker, 1975, p. 260)

The nervousness caused by the strangeness of this new world into which I was thrust accentuated my handicaps, and I found it im-possible to do many things at school which were easy for me at home ... I was always conscious of a nervous tension which did not bother me at home; and though I soon got along there well enough, I hated to go. (Carlson, 1941, pp. 20–21)

...subtly imposing limitations:

While everyone encouraged me on the one hand, they also said I was a dreamer and should not believe in miracles, and, later, that I should not try to do the impossible ... this was one of the subtle modes in which people, through their concern, began to define my capabilities as *they* saw them. They ignored the necessity for me to have the freedom to fail. (French, 1975, p. 237)

The relationship between disability and self-concept has been a topic on which considerable research has been done during the last few years. The final section of this book contains an annotated bibliography of recent research on this topic.

## References

Carlson, E.R. *Born that way*. New York: John Day, 1941.

Dickinson, C. The disabled speak: To learn, to do, to experience, to enjoy. In L. Buscaglia, *The disabled and their parents: A counseling challenge*. Thorofare, NJ: Charles B. Slack, 1975.

French, M. The disabled speak: Stepping stones. In L. Buscaglia, *The disabled and their parents: A counseling challenge*. Thorofare, NJ: Charles B. Slack, 1975.

Keller, H. *The story of my life*. New York: Doubleday, 1961.

# CHAPTER TWO

# The Handicap That Had No Name

**Dale Brown**

My first memory of school is sitting on a hard seat, holding my muscles rigid, trying to concentrate on the teacher's words. "Is this all school is," I think, "just sitting?" I raise my hand.

The teacher calls on me and I stand up. "I'm tired of just sitting here," I tell her.

"Well, Dale, we're big girls now. We sit and we listen."

I sit. I squirm. Soon my seat is slick with sweat and my dress clings damply. The elastic of my underpants cuts. I struggle but I cannot stay still; my body kicks and rocks.

"Dale, please pay attention!" says the teacher.

"You pay money, not attention!" I reply.

The class bursts out laughing.

"You weren't listening," the teacher says. "Now open that book on your desk to page one and mark all the triangles."

I complete the assignment easily.

"Recess time!" calls out our teacher. "Row one may leave."

I jump up happily and follow other children to the cloakroom. It is dark in there. I cannot remember which is my coat. I wait until everyone goes out and take the coat that is left.

The playground is a blacktop area. All the other children talk to each other, play jumprope, chase one another, and swing, but I do not know what to do or how to fit in.

I cannot do anything during gym either. I try and try to bounce a ball but I drop it each time and it takes off halfway across the room. I stare at the other children, effortlessly bouncing their balls. Up and down. Up and down. How do they do it?

"Can't you even try?" the gym teacher yells.

We practice tumbling. I squat but cannot figure out what to do with my hands to make my body roll. The gym teacher grabs my leg and throws me over. It hurts and I do not like the way the world whirls afterwards. The next time he reaches for my leg I kick him. Both he and my teacher are furious. They make me stand in a corner for the rest of the class. I am happier there.

In my recollections, school was a constant struggle that started upon awakening: to find my clothes, to straighten out the dress I tangled, to get my socks on properly, to identify the right shoe for each foot, and to tie the laces. Even managing my body was a struggle. It was hard for me to use my right arm and leg. My head felt heavy and hung down. I shuffled rather than walked and I leaned forward slightly. To move in a straight line, I often walked with one foot on the sidewalk and the other on the grass, or I kept one hand on a wall. When people told me to pick up my feet, I kicked each one up and then stepped down; I could not understand the difference between their way of walking and mine. I always spoke at the top of my lungs because I could not hear myself and "loud" and "soft" had no meaning. Sometimes I smiled with only one side of my mouth. I never blinked and my eyes were often crossed. They wandered randomly, which made it difficult for me to see.

I saw double until the second grade, when I had surgery. Afterwards, my eyes did not work well as a team, causing figure-ground and depth-perception problems. My eyes tracked improperly and it took me a long time to learn to discriminate visually and to focus.

My peers would snap their fingers in front of my eyes and laugh when I did not blink. They held fingers before me and asked, "How many?" I would guess the right answer and think they were trying to help me to learn better. They said I had more "cooties" (germs that could be passed by touching) than everyone combined. One child would touch me and then quickly touch someone else, yelling, "Dale's cooties! I quit!" That child would try to pass along my cooties, too. When we waited at the bus stop, they stood in a circle and I had to stand outside. One boy threw stones at me every day on the way home from the bus.

Luckily, I had one friend, Carol. We played together constantly. Through watching my peers imitate my movements, I learned what I was doing wrong. I started trying to stand up straight with my shoulders back and my head up. I learned to lift my knees when I walked. I liked holding my head up because I could see the world; before, all I had seen was the sidewalk and my feet.

In the fourth grade, Mrs. Johnson was my teacher. She had art class every day and she tacked my pictures on the bulletin board. She also taught creative writing and loved everything I wrote. She helped me to put my poems in a beautiful book bound with red construction paper. Because she let me walk out of class when I became especially restless, I learned to sit still. She gave us very little homework, so I had time to play. I used to practice throwing a ball against the side of the house and catching it. At first, I spent most of the time chasing the ball but soon I was catching it after one bounce.

In the fifth grade, our teacher was Ms. Rhiner. She had red hair and she liked me. But the homework started again. It took me an hour to write a paragraph; often I worked from the time I came home until it was time for bed. I wrote my work letter by letter. I got up from my chair only to get drinks of water. One night, I took a walk instead of doing homework. How I loved the cool evening air! But I felt guilty about that walk for weeks.

I strove to learn. I understood mathematical concepts but my answers were often wrong. "Careless errors," I was told. Yet no matter how carefully I checked my work, my papers earned C's and D's. I could spell, but I wrote too slowly to keep up with the teacher's dictation during tests. "Try harder," I was told. My blackboard work was sloppy so I asked my parents to buy me a chalkboard. I practiced writing on it and found I had to use my arms differently than when I wrote on paper. One day, Ms. Rhiner told me that she would help me with my handwriting in a few weeks. The promise excited me. I practiced harder and harder. I drew lines, big circles, then large letters that covered the entire board. Often I wrote an "a" backwards; I knew that my right side was towards the storage room door but that did not seem to stop me from reversing letters. Sometimes, when I tried to correct an error I would continue to write the letter wrong again and again and again. I had to wait until my chalk broke before I could stop. (Later, I learned to call these incidents "closed circuits of failure.") When I mastered drawing large letters, I practiced making them small.

Then came the day when Ms. Rhiner offered to help me with my handwriting during recess. She told me to write my name on the blackboard. I held the chalk carefully in order not to break it and I drew each letter meticulously. Even the "e," the hardest letter in "Dale," was perfect. I stepped back proudly.

"Why Dale," Ms. Rhiner said, "That's very good! Maybe your basic problem is carelessness."

I was so furious I could not reply. I glared at her and ran outside. "Dale," she called after me, "I'm sorry."

"Carelessness"! I knew that was not my problem. I had worked hard to write well. My handwriting had improved; Ms. Rhiner tore up fewer of my papers. Then what was the problem? Why did I always wiggle in my chair? Why did my muscles have a mind of their own? And why did I write so slowly?

I thought of the story in one of our readers of Glenn Cunningham, the first American to run the four-minute mile. As a child, his legs had been burned in a fire and everyone told him he would never walk again. But he struggled and one day he took his first step. Everyone was amazed. His mother hugged him and the doctor congratulated him. Everyone was happy. He practiced walking and then running. He practiced and practiced until he ran the four-minute mile.

The story inspired me but it also upset me. Suppose when he had risen from his bed and walked, everyone had said, "Well, now you see what you can do if you try." Suppose nobody had hugged him. Would he have been able to achieve his record-breaking feat?

I studied my hands and legs. There was nothing wrong with them but they just did not do what I told them to. I had to practice and practice like Glenn Cunningham but my efforts received no recognition. As an adult, I have words for my confused feelings then: I was jealous of Glenn Cunningham's handicap. It had a name: burned legs. Everyone admired him when he walked. My handicap had no name.

"It helps," I thought, "to pretend I am Glenn Cunningham. When I work hard, I improve. If everyone says I'm not trying, I must not be trying; and because I really am not trying, no one helps me. Nobody ever says 'Good girl' to me. So I'll tell it to myself: *I am a good girl. I am a good girl.*'"

Fifth grade, sixth, seventh, and eighth grade. Time went slowly then. Each second clicked by individually. I hated myself but I never gave up trying. During the summers, I learned how to swim. The Red Cross taught swimming in four two-week classes: Beginner, Intermediate, Junior, and Swimmer. It took me a full summer to complete each class.

I still had trouble in gym. In team games, I had to choose between doing nothing and infuriating my teachers or trying to participate and infuriating my peers. In gymnastics, I had to walk along a balance beam; I often fell off. My peers changed their methods of teasing me: They greeted me in an exaggerated manner or laughed at me behind my back. In eighth grade, my picture was crossed out of many yearbooks.

My grades were poor. I worked hard but my efforts were not recognized or rewarded; most of my grades were C's. One teacher flunked me, explaining, "You're getting an E for effort."

A particular incident stands out in my mind. I was practicing throwing a ball against the wall and catching it. A student teacher came over and said, "Dale, can I help you with that? Let's play catch."

"You'd better not work with me," I said.

"Why not?"

"I'm a very unrewarding child to work with."

"What do you mean?"

"I'm unrewarding." After a silence I explained. "Look, a lot of teachers have given up on me. You'll have more fun with the other kids. I'll just frustrate you."

We stared at each other and then she turned away. I went back to throwing and catching the ball. I had caught it 10 out of 10 times. I took a step backwards to see how well I did.

In retrospect, I know that this young teacher thought she was being helpful. She already had firmly set in her mind the kind of help she wanted to offer but she had no intention of finding out what I needed. I was acting in a determined, disciplined manner, throwing the ball against the wall over and over and catching it, which is rare for a 13-year-old child; she gave me no positive reinforcement for my self-discipline but, instead, interrupted my activity. When she offered to "help" me by playing, her voice was condescending. I knew from past experience with teachers that her patience would not last long. Most teachers had short attention spans, at least when it came to me.

I am also interested, in retrospect, in how I knew that I was an "unrewarding" child. I must have overheard more than one person so describing me—why, otherwise, would the word have come so quickly to my lips?

In French class that year we had to memorize dialogues and recite them. I used to wait in dread for my turn because when I stood up all I could do was stutter. I was given a D in the course and the counselor called me in to discuss the grade.

"I can't memorize the dialogues," I explained. "I practiced every night; I read them over and over, but it does no good. The words fly out of my mind. It must be a mental block."

We spent an hour together and got nowhere. Finally, she said, "Dale, can't you just pretend the dialogues are words to a song?"

"I can't memorize songs either. Every Christmas I try to learn the carols again. I listen, I look at the words, I have friends say the words and I repeat them, but it doesn't help."

We sat silently. How close we were to the core of my problems! However, at that time, the theory that would have explained me to myself did not exist. Although the counselor could offer me nothing, I thanked her and left.

My high school years also went slowly. The teachers were less alert and less caring, perhaps because there were so many of us in each class and they had troubles of their own. For example, one English teacher was assigned to teach geography. Our math teacher, who had never learned the new math, was told to teach it; every day, before class, the department head tutored her for the next day's lesson. Everything in my life was such a struggle for me at that time that I just stopped struggling to do well in school.

My vision was a problem. Things seemed to melt together so that it was hard for me to find the lock on my locker or a book on a shelf. I had no social skills. In group projects, such as cooking or putting up a tent, I did not know how to help. And the flow of conversation was difficult for me to master. It took months of watching before I understood how people interrupted each other. Even so, I could not learn how to use the signals with ease.

When I was admitted to Pitzer College (Los Angeles), I was excited by the prospect of a new beginning. I determined to study hard. I hoped to make new friends; certainly my high school reputation could not follow me. Yet other students still shied away from me. I often ate alone in the large noisy cafeteria because it was difficult for me to recognize familiar faces at a distance while I balanced my tray. People said I ignored them when they called to me. I made a disciplined effort to make friends. I kept a notebook of people's names, classes, and other information and I reviewed the lists each night. I learned to tell whether I was speaking loudly or softly by holding a hand to my throat. Finally, I found some friends. We always sat at the same table in the cafeteria and frequently we were joined by other students. My group interaction skills improved but most students thought of me as a "weirdo." I could not understand why.

Academically, the college was difficult. In some of my classes I could not seem to hold the necessary facts in my head. By the end of the first semester, I had dropped one course, and had two incompletes and one B. The next semester I not only had to carry on my normal course work but, also, to complete the incompletes. I consulted with upperclassmen and chose easier classes. I gave up my attempts to socialize and worked day and night. By the end of the year, I had A's and one B.

I applied to Antioch College because of their work-study program and their nontraditional approach to education. When I was accepted, I hoped once again to make a new start. The first night there, my roommate Sandy and I talked until morning. On the way to breakfast, we were joined by Betty, who lived across the hall, and several other dorm residents. While we were eating, Sandy said, "You know Dale, it's funny, but it was easier talking to you last night. Your staring bugs me!"

"Me, too!" said Betty. "I really like you, though. Is something wrong with your eyes?"

"I think so," I replied, "But I don't know what."

"Lots of people stare," said Allen. "It doesn't bother me at all."

"You're not sitting across from her," said Sandy. "I feel as if she's looking right through me."

After breakfast, I went to my Principles of Education class. There were six of us. The professor began an exciting discussion and I had a lot to say, but I could not seem to get my words in. In the middle of the class, the professor said, "Dale, what's happening? You start to talk and then stop yourself."

"I don't want to interrupt anyone," I told him.

He said, "This sounds like a group problem."

The other five members of the class explained that they expected me to interrupt them and they were interested in my views. "How can we help?" the professor asked.

"Well, will you call on me when you want me to speak?"

"Okay. I'll try to remember. Anyone else can call on you, too. Now, how did you react to Tom's comments on free education?"

Antioch College enabled me to socialize. Many students had been through encounter and sensitivity groups and they gave and received feedback freely. Group projects were common. I learned the things about myself that bothered people and I corrected them. I constantly reminded myself to blink and to move my eyes from person to person as each spoke. The movements confused me visually but they made other people more comfortable. I stopped jumping at the slightest sound and turned my eyes and head towards what I wanted to see. In fact, I became tense because of the constant awareness of my body. It was worth it because my peers avoided me less.

We went to school all year in four alternating quarters of work and study. Jobs could be taken anywhere in the world. Thus, every three months, my peer group changed. As I improved, my reputation did not drag me back into old behaviors. I mastered conversational signals, after several years, and could speak without interrupting other people. Yet, I always had to strain to understand and keep up. I had to think about what came naturally to others. And my handicap still had no name. There was no apparent reason for the effort I had to make.

Things came to a head when I was employed as a factory worker at an electronics assembly company. I knew that I would be working on tasks requiring excellent coordination but I felt ready; my vision and motor abilities had improved. I was optimistic that the job would help me to overcome my handicap.

On my first day, Marie, my supervisor, led me into a small rectangular room where two long tables stood in the middle, workbenches were placed against three walls, and floor-to-ceiling shelves lined the fourth wall. Large machines sat on one of the center tables and an oven stood near the door. Marie sat me down at one of the workbenches and started instructing me. When I pulled out a pad to make notes, she objected and I put the pad away. She gave me a razor blade and showed me my task.

I was supposed to strip the encasing rubber and insulation from three wires and then to twist the copper strands slightly. No matter how hard I tried, and despite Marie's efforts to help me, I could not find the right amount of pressure to put on the blade. I cut my fingers again and again.

After four hours, Marie said, "Dale, you've caused too much scrap. You can try again tomorrow. Right now, I'm giving you another job—putting together probes." She took me to a winch. Once again, I took out my notebook and again she objected because "it will take forever if you do."

She picked up a metal rod from the table. "Now you put this bar on the winch"—she turned the knob on the side of the winch—"then you screw this top on." The "top" was a large silver ball.

"How did you get the rod to fit in the winch?" I asked.

"I just explained that!"

"Well, I probably wasn't listening while you turned that knob because I needed to see how you did it."

Her face grew grim. She went through the procedure again with a running commentary. When the probe was assembled she stood aside and said, "Now you do it."

I had no idea where to begin. I had forgotten the first thing she said. She prompted me, "You put the rod in the winch."

My eyes, however, could not find the metal rods on the silvery table. When I asked where they were, she retorted, "Right in front of your nose!" She lifted one from the pile in front of me.

I put the rod in the winch and turned the knob. "You're loosening it!" I nodded and switched directions. After 30 minutes of my errors, she let me take notes. Then it took another half hour while I drew my diagrams. When we finished, she exclaimed, "It took me an hour to teach you what should have taken 10 minutes." I used my diagrams to remember how to put 20 probes together. Marie informed me that it took the average worker half the time.

I was determined not to become an outcast. I sat straight and proud. I ignored putdowns. I not only avoided verbal replies but made sure my body language remained unaffected. When Marie taught me, I kept my voice matter-of-fact, although I knew my questions were unreasonable. I apologized calmly and took responsibility for my mistakes. I was proud as I improved, yet I remained significantly slower and less accurate than the other workers.

Huge metal racks to heat the probes were on many work tables. One day, Marie said, "Go to the second shelf from the top of the third set from the left side. On the right of the shelf, there are some plastic drawers and on the right compartment of the bottom drawer, you'll find about 100 bolts. Sit next to Barbara and help her. She'll tell you what she's doing."

I walked towards the shelves, trying to hold the instructions in my mind.

"Dale!" Marie said.

I was so startled I banged into a rack. It was hot.

I looked at my arm. A patch of skin turned red, then white. Then the pain hit.

"Which set of plastic drawers?" I asked Marie.

"Dale, what happened to your arm?" asked one of the women.

"It got burned when I banged into that rack."

"Let me see it," said Marie. "That may be serious. Better go to the nurse." As I left, she said, "You didn't even say 'Ouch'!" She sounded puzzled.

On the way to the nurse, I thought about it. "If you are a klutz, pain is just part of life. You learn not to say anything and hope people will ignore your clumsiness. What hurts you makes others laugh." As a child, I had fallen on floors and banged into walls; I had learned not to react so no one would make fun of me. Then I thought, "Whatever my problem is, it can't be psychological. I don't hate myself this much."

The nurse put oil and bandages on the burn. She said "It looks like you'll have a scar for about three years. Maybe longer."

When I returned to my unit, Barbara showed me how to put the bolts on the ceramics. It was easy and I could think as I worked. Something was seriously wrong and everyone sensed it. Something besides my vision and lack of coordination was causing problems. I decided to list my mistakes. I wrote them on the pad I used for job numbers and Marie's instructions. Strangely enough, this activity earned me respect from some coworkers. I resolved not to look at my list until my time was up.

On my last day of work, Marie said, "I guess you got mad at us sometimes and we got mad at you. But I really hope it wasn't too bad."

"I hope it wasn't too bad for you," I replied. "Thank you for your patience."

I left feeling relieved, upset, and guilty.

In my apartment I studied the error list. Over half my mistakes involved hearing. Hearing! I knew that my vision and touch were off. I knew I was clumsy and had no sense of direction. But I had assumed that my hearing was safe. I knew then that I could trust none of my senses. I was depressed for days. When my depression did not lift, I made an appointment at the college counseling center.

"I had some problems on my last job," I explained to the counselor, "and I hoped talking to an adult might help." I told her everything that had happened, and showed her my list of errors. "My boss always yelled at me. She said it took me too long to learn things. I was so clumsy I cut my fingers with the razor blades and burned myself severely." I showed her the scar. "Anyway, I'm here because I don't know what's going on. My unconscious mind can't hate me this much! I feel upset, but I don't feel crazy."

She asked me many questions. Finally, she said, "It sounds to me as if you might have perceptual problems. Your hearing difficulties sound like auditory sequencing problems."

"Auditory sequencing problems?" I questioned.

"Problems in hearing sounds in the right order. That's why you always have to write down what you hear. Our staff can give you the Wepman test of auditory discrimination." (I scored in the lowest five percent in my ability to hear sounds over background noise.)

The counselor continued, "Your visual and auditory problems and inability to tell right from left sound like perceptual problems, trouble taking in information through your senses. You really fit the constellation well. Why don't you read a textbook on learning disabilities? Most of them have a section on perception. I wish there was more I could suggest, but there are really no tests for people your age."

At the library the next day, I found that there was no catalogue category for learning disabilities, so I went to the special education stacks. I found plenty of material on physical and mental handicaps but nothing I could identify as my area of concern. After several hours of browsing, I came upon *Psychology of Exceptional Children and Youth* (Cruikshank, 1963). One chapter was called "Psychological Characteristics of Brain-Injured Children" by Cruickshank & Paul. I had to read it several times before I could fully absorb the contents.

The characteristics described by the authors appeared to be a problem-by-problem profile of myself. *Hyperactivity* ("always in motion and ... always double time"). *Hyperdistractibility* ("inability to focus attention selectively on one major aspect of a situation ... overresponse to external stimuli and ... overresponse to internal stimuli"). I thought, "So that was why they always said I wasn't paying attention!" I looked at the wall in front of me. I had learned always to study in isolated places where I was not distracted by the passage of people and the rustling of pages.

*Perseveration* ("the lack of impuse control of a motor act of some kind"). I remembered writing the wrong letter on the blackboard over and over and over again—"closed failure circuits."

*Lability of affect* (emotional instability; overraction). The chapter described a 10-year-old girl who burst into tears "accompanied by loud sobs" when she accomplished a task upon which she had been engaged for several days. I was not surprised. "Maybe she had been working on it for months which the researcher didn't know about," I thought. "Even the researcher didn't understand that it was normal for her to cry; these handicaps can be hard and frustrating."

*Motor dysfunction* ("difficulties in gross and fine motor movements ... the inability to move one's body in a synchronized and integrated fashion"). No wonder I was such a klutz!

Later, the chapter explained the perceptual distortions that afflict the brain-injured child: "figure ground disturbances ... the brain-injured child is unable to attend to the figure. The background becomes highly distractible to the child and he is forced to respond to it." I wondered if that explained why my vision seemed to melt things together and why I had trouble seeing a dish on a shelf or a knob on a piece of equipment.

*Auditory problems* ("sounds run together and are not integrated into a meaningful sequence or pattern").

All my problems had been described in the 20 pages of the chapter. I was not crazy. I had an identifiable medical syndrome. I was not alone any more. Looking back, I could identify the attitudes which had helped my development and those which had hindered it. I had not been diagnosed as a child. It is quite likely at that time that school personnel and doctors did not know about my minimal brain dysfunction. This fact, perhaps, helps to explain the swiftness and harshness of people's judgments. My low performance was always seen in terms of "carelessness" and "not trying," an attitude that led to a workload which was heavy almost to the point of cruelty. Because I was funny-looking and not socially adept, my peers had teased me a great deal. The same elements that made me the butt of my peers created problems for me with some teachers. As I grew older, the overt teasing stopped but people avoided me.

People with a visible disability are given positive reinforcement for what they can do. We admire the person in a wheelchair who travels around the country in a motorized van or the blind television talk-show host; the blind person who learns cane mobility receives positive reinforcement from the teacher. On the other hand, people with invisible handicaps are expected to attain the norm without effort. They rarely receive credit for their attempts; they are criticized for having trouble in the first place.

I recommend that parents and teachers of learning disabled/minimal brain damaged children talk frankly about the handicap and its manifestations and express confidence that the children can handle it. It is important to recognize and reinforce the discipline it takes a person to overcome this handicap. Ironically, a direct challenge (i.e., "You will never learn to drive a car") can be more motivating than the serene belief that one can achieve something easily (i.e., "You could read that if only you tried a little harder"). A helpful approach when an LD student is having difficulty with a task like math might be to say "I know you're having trouble with that math. I like the way you're working hard at it. Do you think you can finish seven problems by the end of the period? That way, you would do even better than yesterday!" Sincere approval is very motivating.

Specific feedback, whether negative or positive, helped me. For example, at Antioch, for the first time, people stopped and analyzed what it was about me that bothered them. Sandy, who told me not to stare, and my factory supervisor, who let me know exactly how I compared with other workers, gave me useful information. Lenora Johnson, my fourth-grade teacher, was the person who started my career as a writer.

It helped me when my professor in Principles of Education stopped the class to find out why I was starting to speak and then stopping myself. What was happening was that as soon as I got the words ready to say, someone else was talking. The behavior had occurred in many groups, but that professor was the first person to encourage me to participate. He also encouraged everyone in the class to help me, setting the stage for acceptance rather than rejection.

The counselor who tried to understand why I got a D in French gave me sympathetic attention which was helpful. It is too bad neither of us were able to generalize that I had trouble remembering what I heard.

My parents never lost faith in me and gave me a tremendous amount of support. My mother taught me how to read. Despite my many hair-raising escapades, she guided me with a firm hand but never overprotected me. My father helped to teach me how to drive. He helped me to develop social skills by role-playing critical incidents.

Perhaps the counselor who told me that she thought I had perceptual problems was the most helpful character in my story. Learning about my problem changed me from a person who hated herself to someone who likes herself and knows that she is struggling with a real handicap. My problems have not changed but my attitude has.

### Reference

Cruickshank, W. (Ed.). *Psychology of exceptional children and youth* (2nd ed.). Englewood Cliffs, NJ: Prentice Hall, 1963.

# CHAPTER THREE

# Orthopedically Disabled: Determination on Wheels

## Diane Lattin

**M**any of us who are now adults, but were once students with disabilities, have seen attitudes about special education change through the years—even our own.

My perspectives on attitudes and attitude change in special education are based on several factors: my experience as a disabled student, my work as a counselor at a school for handicapped children, and the knowledge I have gained as a result of my work at the President's Committee on Employment of the Handicapped. Changes in myself as I have grown as a disabled person, changes in the law, and changes in the world around me have broadened or altered my perspectives. Some of my original beliefs, however, remain unchanged, and, in fact, have been strengthened.

My perspectives as an orthopedically disabled adult and the changes in my attitudes can be more completely understood by examining the education I had and my experience before and during that time.

I became ill at the age of 9 and got progressively sicker, until surgery, for a benign tumor inside my spinal cord rapidly growing to my brain, left me totally disabled at the age of 12. Until the time of my illness, I was an active tomboy. My favorite toy was not a doll, but a basketball. I loved to ride my bike "no hands" down the big hill near our house; and at the time I became ill, I was well into horseback riding lessons, just learning to jump—an activity in which I found joy unlike anything I had ever known. (After I became paralyzed, it was the only thing I really missed in my life. To my delight, a few years ago, I learned of a special program that included disabled people and I was able to start horseback riding again.)

Most of all, however, I enjoyed my friends. A large park at the end of our block attracted kids in abundance every day. With little supervision, we played for hours, sometimes actively, sometimes just sitting under the large trees—trading cards or playing jacks, describing the kind of horse we wanted to own someday, hunting four-leaf clovers— doing the nothing things children do. These nothing things were the most important part of my life.

When I say that I suffered no true sadness on finding out that I was to be disabled for the rest of my life, I am sure that some eyebrows will go up in disbelief and protest will be voiced: "You were *that* active a child and becoming paralyzed didn't bother you? That can't be possible!"

Nevertheless, I stick by my statement that I suffered no loss, for it is a true one. There is a very simple reason for my matter-of-fact acceptance of the situation. Due to the rarity of my illness, my condition was misdiagnosed by several doctors. Thus, I spent three years in partial and whole body casts. Not only was I unable to take part in the activities I loved, but, I could not even get out of bed most of the time. Often I was too sick to see my friends. Worst of all was the continuous pain. The doctors' diagnoses did not account for such pain and suffering so they said I "made it up" to get attention. Because I was made to feel so guilty for having pain, often I suffered it silently, fearing the wrath of the doctors and the confused, frightened looks of my parents if I complained. And each month, my condition got worse.

When my parents, who always believed my pain was real, finally found a doctor who correctly diagnosed my illness, I was operated on within three days. Usually, parents try to protect their children from the harsh realities of life. Perhaps my parents thought that after all the years of pain I deserved to know that I was really as sick as I had felt, that the other doctors had been wrong but this one could be trusted. For whatever their reasons, my parents gave me a wonderful present before my surgery: They told me the truth.

The truth was that without surgery, I would die very soon. There was a less than 50-50 chance I would survive the surgery and if I did, I would be paralyzed the rest of my life. But my parents promised that after the surgery healed, the pain, the terrible pain that had been with me constantly, would be gone forever. To me, that was all that mattered.

When I found myself alive after surgery and when the pain gradually disappeared to nothing within a few weeks, I never looked back with any sense of loss. I was on my way to recovery. I was without pain. Soon I could rejoin my friends. That I would do so in a wheelchair seemed unimportant.

Perhaps because of the way I came to disability (I knew I would be a paraplegic), my reaction to it differed from that of many other children. Each of us reacts to situations in unique ways. I share the prelude and my reaction to disability because it may help in understanding my perspective toward the education of disabled children.

My education as a disabled student began when I was 12 years old. Recovering from the surgery which left me a paraplegic required that I get two years of schooling through home instruction. However, at the beginning of the ninth grade it was determined that I could return to a school setting. A special education school was suggested—a suggestion quickly rejected by our family. My parents saw to it that I went to a school with "normal" children. No special schools for me. Other handicapped people might need special help, but not me. Any help I needed would come from the able-bodied teenagers I went to school with.

Today, I am embarrassed at my motivation for going to a regular rather than a special education school. My reason was that I was not a freak and would not go to school with a bunch of freaks. Nature had played a trick on my body but my spirit was never "afflicted." In my mind's eye, I was still as agile and able as I had been previously.

When I went to school, I learned more about my life and I educated people in ways that could not be gotten from a textbook. We learned together, my able-bodied classmates and I, what it is like to live with a disability in an able-bodied world. There were stairs in my high school. I was still wearing braces then and my class schedule was arranged so that each semester I took half my classes upstairs and half downstairs, going either up or down at lunchtime; thus I had to make only one trip a day up and down the stairs. It was a tiring, time-consuming process, lifting or lowering myself on braces and crutches on two somewhat narrow flights while my wheelchair was bounced separately ahead of me.

The school had no bathroom which I could use. This situation caused some embarrassing moments for me and required that my mother be almost constantly on call to pick me up and drive me home to the bathroom, if necessary.

Going to school in a building unsuited to my physical needs placed what I now know were grossly unfair requirements on me and my family. This did not seem true at the time. My parents believed that all the problems had to be endured because they had a child with a disability who was going to a regular school. And so did I.

As I became more comfortable in my surroundings, I was not against using my disability and at times my friends and I would skip classes (it was a great gimmick too, for my able-bodied friends who were "helping" me), but it never would have occurred to me to ask for special favors. In fact, I graduated without an academic diploma because, with the way we had to schedule my classes, I could not get all the math credits I needed. Neither my parents nor I ever thought of asking that a class be rescheduled to a different classroom for my benefit.

A friend I had known before my illness probably contributed more to my independence than anything else. When I returned to school after several years of home instruction, she was there to help me out. It was good for her too. She lived nearby, so we took her to school in our car, which meant that she could sleep late and did not have to rush to catch an early school bus. She used to help me up the steps, assist me in keeping my balance, and recruit other friends to help get the wheelchair upstairs.

The arrangement worked for a time. In time, though, she began to tire of her responsibility, for it often kept her from doing something else she wanted to do. One day, when she did not show up, I asked another friend to help. While my old friend faded away, new friends took her place; with growing confidence, I was not uncomfortable in asking anyone who was going the same way for a little help.

I learned that it was okay to ask for help. As long as I did not impose unduly on one person, people did not mind helping. In fact, because they were curious about this single handicapped person in their school, students asked questions when they helped me. So I learned that it was okay to talk about my disability and to ask questions of other people in return. I met a lot of people going up and down those stairs.

My parents and I saw to it that I did more than go to classes. I also attended football games, plays, and parties. I joined clubs and worked on the newspaper. A lot of extra effort was required from my family but I was always a participant, never just an observer.

When I was 16 and eligible for a driver's license, a whole new dimension was added to my life: freedom. With a car equipped with hand controls, I took over my mother's duties. My car was a big hit at the local drive-in because my friends and I could drive around in it with our legs hanging out the windows.

Going to high school in seemingly inaccessible surroundings was such a success that I did the same thing in college. I had become more accepting of my own disability, but I was still not too sure about anyone else's. So I rejected the idea of attending the University of Illinois which, I was told, had special facilities. It still sounded too much like "birds of a feather flock together" for me to feel comfortable with the idea. I went to school in my own area and commuted from home.

Once in college, I gave up my leg braces and now people carried me and my wheelchair together up flights of stairs. I still would not consider asking for special privileges. In the first place, I knew the college had accepted me with some reservations; I was afraid that if I caused problems they would dump me. (Somehow, to me, asking the school to change a class would have seemed like asking for special favors, but expecting my classmates to carry me up flights of stairs seemed like no imposition at all.)

When I graduated from college I moved into my own apartment. I was now totally independent. I had done what I knew I could do: I had accepted the able-bodied world on its terms. The acceptance was not without a heavy price; I spent many unnecessary months in the hospital because I abused my body trying to do everything my peers did. Also, the sacrifices required of my family now seem unreasonable. In order for me to live a "normal" life, they had to live a completely abnormal one, dealing daily with many unnecessary problems.

Although I am sorry now for my reasons, I will be grateful forever that I did not go to a special education school. The segregated system of education that existed then and still exists for disabled children makes us cripples, I believe, more than anything else. It shelters and protects handicapped children from the real world and it makes able-bodied children feel exactly the way I did—that special schools are for freaks.

My education in a regular school setting was essential in preparing me to meet the demands that all of us must face when we finish our education and enter the job world. But I would do many things differently if I were going to school now, based on what I have learned. My attitudes toward what I can expect of other people—family, friends, persons in positions of authority—have changed. Most important, my perceptions of other people who are disabled have changed also.

After I became disabled, I had the idea that I was, somehow, a unique handicapped person. My basic knowledge of handicapped people came from such things as telethons so I saw all handicapped people as pitiful creatures who could only survive in this world with the benevolent help of those who offered them charity. I knew I was not like that and, therefore, assumed I must be unique. Because of these feelings, I was absolutely certain that I did not want to be put in a school with these pitiful children who were so helpless they could not function in a regular school.

Obviously, my perception of disabled people and myself as unique among them has changed as I have gotten to know other disabled people. However, my feelings at the time I was going to school delayed for many years my involvement with anyone who was disabled.

There were, perhaps, three or four other handicapped people at my college. I was the only one in my high school. Apparently, we all had the same feelings about handicapped people, which is why we had chosen an inaccessible school where there were so few disabled students. We avoided each other like the plague. Any suggestion by another student that we should meet so-and-so, "who's in a wheelchair, too," was met with thundering silence.

One of the other disabled students at college with me was blind. Because of our work, we have now become friends. We both look back at our college careers with some amusement. He now uses a white cane to help him find his way around, but when he was in college he too was intent on proving that he was unique and refused to use a cane or dog guide.

As he explains it, "I spent four years running into buildings, tripping up curbs, and bumping into people, all the while feeling that I was impressing people because I didn't have to use a cane to get around."

My situation was similar. I spent my school years imposing on everyone to get me up and down stairs while feeling that I was independent because I did not have to go to a school especially designed to meet my needs.

Since then I have learned a little bit more about independence and my rights as a human being. The idea that I could ask friends and family for favors but could not ask institutions to reschedule classes, widen doors, or put in ramps has definitely been altered. The fact that disabled people do need some special accommodations to give them equal opportunities is no longer perceived by me as some kind of personal failure to accommodate to the "real" world.

It was not until I became a counselor at a school for handicapped children that I learned something about the special education I had so assiduously avoided as a student. The school where I worked had children in grades kindergarten through 12. All the things that had been denied me as a student were available: transportation, ramps, bathrooms, desks (I always worked on my lap), games everyone could play, and students and teachers who understood and did not ask embarrassing questions.

Essentially, the children were no different from their able-bodied peers. Some were troublemakers, scholars, flirts, or athletes; some wanted to be doctors, policemen, baseball players, or nurses; some had parents who cared, drank too much, came to meetings, worked as volunteers or made excuses. These children were individuals with the same problems and dreams that all children have. Their handicaps were not additional problems but just parts of them, like their brown eyes, blond hair, excess weight, overdone make-up, blue jeans, or pimples.

However, because of what they had been taught about themselves by the rest of the world, it was apparent that these children were comfortable in a way they never could have been in a regular school. An epileptic seizure caused no comment; wheelchair spills evoked laughter; and cerebral palsied speech patterns were commonly heard and, therefore, readily understood. In this psychological climate, in an environment that had no architectural barriers, an atmosphere of security that fostered learning was created.

Something else was apparent to me however; this sheltered, protected environment with no questions and no rejection was not the real world. This school was giving the children an academic or vocational education but it was teaching them absolutely nothing about the problems they would meet once they left their parents' homes and the school.

The experience of working at the school for the handicapped served to solidify my long-held belief that segregated, special schools are in some important ways detrimental to children with disabilities.

I learned from talking to the teachers and other counselors that many of the students who graduated went to work in sheltered workshops or in mundane jobs they did not like. Very few—almost none—went on to college. A few went to training schools. Many did nothing. Those who did nothing had tried a job and failed. Or they had been afraid to take a job in a place away from their friends where they did not know anyone. Of course, some had been unable to get jobs. The group that saddened me most were those who tried and failed or were afraid to try at all. Their special school had not prepared them for failure or for a hostile climate in which they might have to prove themselves.

Another thing I learned could have been a forecast of what would happen after graduation. On several occasions, we attempted to place students who were not severely disabled in a regular school setting. One teenage girl with a deformed arm was absolutely refused attendance by the principal of the regular school, because "She would be too much of a distraction for the other children."

A young boy on braces and crutches went to a junior high school across the street from the special school. He rode the special school bus to and from school but went to classes at the regular school. Because he had to ride the special bus, he could not take part in any after-school activities. Although he had been a good student at the special school, he began to fail in his studies at the new school. He was obviously unhappy and missed his old friends; he was unable to make new ones. A few months later he returned "home" at his own request.

We made a few attempts to place students and only one succeeded. A teenage boy who had hemophilia was sent to a regular high school. Aside from being small for his age and having the possibility of bleeding accidents, he was not visibly disabled. (In fact, his placement in a special school as well as the placement of several other students seemed more precautionary than necessary.) After his placement in the regular program, which was completely separate from the special school, including riding a regular bus, he came back a couple of times to visit his friends, somewhat like a conquering hero. His visits became less and less frequent and soon he was completely absorbed into the regular school system. The last I heard of him, he was in college on a scholarship.

If the teachers had had the proper training, and if support services had been available, the students who failed would probably have "mainstreamed" easily. However, as a counselor I encountered a resistance factor I had not expected. The resistance was from the parents of disabled children and was one of the major reasons we made so few attempts at outside placement. This parental resistance might also have been a significant factor in the failure of most of the placements we made.

I suppose my surprise at parental resistance to placement in regular schools was because my parents had been so adamant about my placement in a regular school setting. It never occurred to me that, given a choice, parents would prefer that their children go to a special school. I had thought it was something that was forced upon them, as it was nearly forced upon our family.

In fact, most of the parents were afraid that their children would be hurt physically and emotionally by the regular school experience. However, more important than what they saw as the risk of unnecessary injury was the fear that their children would be taunted and made fun of and would not be accepted by their able-bodied peers. They felt that the least that could be expected in the hostile surroundings of the regular school was that their children would be totally left out and ignored and would have no friends.

My experiences as a disabled student did not justify any of these fears. I remember that in grade school, when I was still an able-bodied student, one young boy, whose mother worked at the school, used braces and crutches as a result of polio. As far as I know, other than the fact that his mother drove him to and from school, he was treated just like the rest of us. I vaguely remember his lumbering down the hall on his braces and helping the teacher to keep score at the basketball games. Perhaps he was lonely and left out, but I do not think so. I remember that he had a lovely voice and sang a solo one year in our Christmas pageant.

One thing he had going for him, which I had also but which many disabled children lack, is that aside from our obvious disabilities we looked completely normal. We were not disfigured in any way. Perhaps a speech problem, disfigurement, or spasticity causes more discomfort for able-bodied children and they are more apt to mistreat such disabled children. Obviously, to overcome this possibility, more severely disabled children must have concomitant amounts of support.

The parents I met as a counselor were absolutely certain that their children could not make it in a regular school and they imparted these fears to their children. Arguments over what this attitude meant to the children's future when they finished school could not sway the parents. They wanted their children's happiness in the present rather than the future, and they felt that outside of the protected environment of the special school it was threatened.

I feel that by their attitudes and actions these parents were creating a self-fulfilling prophecy. By segregating their children and instilling them with their parental fears, they were making the children themselves feel different. Consequently, in the presence of able-bodied children, these disabled children were insecure and withdrawn and presented themselves awkwardly. During the time I was a counselor, we had some "mixed" functions with other schools which were not terribly successful. The disabled children were awkward and the two groups did not mix well.

Perhaps, on these occasions, there was too much teacher-parent pressure and intervention. Maybe if the children had been entirely on their own, things would have been better. However, I think that the feelings the children had developed as a result of their segregation played the biggest part. The disabled children had a concept of themselves as unwanted by able-bodied children. The able-bodied children probably had the same feelings I had about disabled children before I became one of them: Because these children were too "sick" to go to regular school, they were to be pitied and treated kindly. You could not play with them and talk to them like other kids. You could hurt them if you touched them and, of course, since they were cripples, it was unkind to remind them of what they could not do by talking about baseball or the newest dance craze. They were the poster and telethon children you gave your pennies to help.

The able-bodied and disabled children who, in reality, were so much alike, had been taught by parents, media, and the segregated system of education that they were totally different from one another. Each passing year solidified these teachings; when these students graduated there was a chasm of difference that could never be bridged. Consequently, disabled children who were the cute poster children whom people wanted to help often grew up to be the disabled adults whom no one wanted to hire.

These children had been educated in a way no one had intended. Disabled children had been educated to believe that those who did not know their needs would reject them. Able-bodied children who had had no education in the capabilities of disabled people did reject them.

When I came to work for the President's Committee on Employment of the Handicapped, it seemed that my beliefs were borne out by the available factual information. The 1970 census, for the first time, provided information on people who were disabled. One of the things the census showed was that one out of every 11 people in the United States between the ages of 16 and 64 (the population that the census measured) was disabled. Of that disabled population, 52% had incomes of less than $3,000 a year. More important, in terms of education, the census showed that 47% of the disabled population never completed high school and only 9% ever finished college.

Although there was no specific information to substantiate my belief that segregated education affected schooling or income, it is clear that at the time of the 1970 census, most children were educated in a segregated environment. Only a few of us had parents who defied the odds and the system and fought for regular school placement.

I have met some people who have rejected me professionally because of my disability. Some have treated me callously socially because of my wheelchair. However, I had experienced all that long ago when I had the eternal optimism and resilience that blesses only the young. So, as an adult, I am not devastated by these reactions. More than that, as a student I learned that just as many or more people see me as their equal.

This sense of security means that I now feel no need to be eternally grateful to those persons who recognize the fact of equality. In my wheelchair, I stand on an equal footing with my able-bodied and disabled friends and coworkers.

# CHAPTER FOUR

# I'm A Person, Not A Wheelchair! Problems of Disabled Adolescents

**Michael Winter**
**Dorothy DeSimone**

The life of any teenager is marked by a great deal of frustration, uncertainty, and vulnerability. Adolescents must learn to deal with continual physical change and newly emerging sexual feelings. The development of the self-image reaches an especially critical stage during adolescence; hence, teenagers' feelings about themselves are tenuous and uncertain. Social attitudes, particularly as they are reflected in the attitudes of family members, friends, teachers, and other significant persons, profoundly influence adolescents' self-images. They see themselves mainly through the reactions and judgments of other people.

Negative attitudes that devalue the individual have a destructive influence on even the strongest personality. Consider, then, the effect they must have on disabled teenagers who, usually, have not had time or opportunity to develop secure self-concepts. Limited by the effects of disabilities on mind and body, disabled teenagers are restricted much more severely by attitudes that often compel them to measure themselves in unfair and unrealistic terms. They may be expected either to overachieve—to assume the role of "super-crip"—or to accomplish very little in the normal scheme of things.

Disabilities often become the central focus in the lives of such youngsters and the major factor around which their total personalities are evaluated. Physical limitations are used to gauge their mental capacities, emotional stability, psychological health, and even moral character. The mere presence of a wheelchair, which provides some disabled persons with greater mobility and freedom, can also subject them to painful personal devaluation. They melt into and become part of the inanimate object thoughtlessly referred to as "that wheelchair." "Get that wheelchair out of the way!" is a phrase often directed at disabled persons in public places. The fact that there is a person sitting in the chair is ignored or not recognized. It is not uncommon for disabled teenagers to go to parties and to be told to stay in corners so "they won't be in anyone's way."

However difficult adolescence is for the nondisabled youngster, it is even more difficult for a teenager with a disability. True, there are many similarities between the difficulties of nondisabled and disabled teenagers but, for the latter, ordinary problems are magnified and frustrations and uncertainties are more frequent and intense. The relationships of disabled teenagers with their parents are frequently marked by differential treatment and an unusual degree of overprotection. A child who receives too much help may become overly dependent on family members; preferential treatment may cause a youngster to expect such treatment from others for the rest of his or her life. Overprotection fosters a sheltered existence in which children are given little or no opportunity to develop the skills essential for successful daily living.

Most disabled adolescents are aware that the presence of disabilities makes them different and that therefore they are treated differently. They have many questions about the nature and effects of their disabilities which may not be adequately answered: "Will I always have to use a wheelchair?" "Can I get married and have children?" "Will I be able to get a job?" The usual difficulties in communication between adolescents and their parents are compounded when the youngsters are disabled. In addition, parents frequently do not have adequate information to answer important questions and they may be wary of seeking the truth. If they feel uncomfortable talking about their children's disabilities, they may try to ignore or conceal the realities of the disabilities. This situation also tends to be found among other family members and society in general. Thus, disabled children learn that their disabilities are unpleasant and discomforting at the least and shameful and embarrassing at the worst. They learn to refrain from speaking about their disabilities, although the need to do so is urgent. Questions, consequently, remain unanswered and feelings are buried deep inside.

All adolescents have difficulty sorting out and expressing their feelings, but disabled teenagers seem to have even greater difficulty. In 1978, the Center for Independent Living at Berkeley, California held rap sessions where disabled teenagers were provided a forum for discussing their feelings with family members and friends. The sessions were led by disabled adults.

The teenagers who participated were very reluctant to talk about their problems or to express their feelings, especially their negative feelings. One youth said that his family seemed to take it for granted that he was happy and contented but rarely asked him how he actually felt. They failed to recognize his need to communicate as an individual.

Denial or suppression of feelings seems to be particularly common in the area of sexuality. Society tends to think of disabled persons as asexual or unable to function sexually. Adults, uncomfortable enough when faced with the sexual curiosity of nondisabled youngsters, find their discomfort greatly increased when they are confronted with the emerging sexuality of disabled teenagers. The disabled adolescents in the group felt they were not expected to have sexual feelings or to be the object of other people's desires. Dealing with these feelings was especially painful for these young people. They asked such questions as "Are my feelings normal?" "Will I ever be able to perform sexually?" "Will I ever have the opportunity to experiment, to be alone with myself or another person long enough to express my feelings physically?" Disabled teenagers tend to have less opportunity for privacy than do other young people, yet their need to be alone with friends is the same. Disabled adults who participated in the project remembered their own lack of privacy during adolescence; being alone on a date was a virtual impossibility.

The teenagers in our group seemed to have a limited social life. Those who attended special schools often had to travel long distances and most had to leave for home right after classes. Extracurricular activities, consequently, were severely limited for them. The friends they made at school usually did not live in their neighborhoods. If they wished to visit these friends or to be visited, they had to depend on family members for transportation. Limited physical mobility also prevents disabled teenagers from getting around freely in their own neighborhoods. Making friends with other teenagers who live nearby is not an easy task. Teenagers who have been "mainstreamed" into regular classrooms often have had little experience in relating to nondisabled peers.

A female student recently mainstreamed into a regular high school needed some assistance to eat her lunch; sometimes she spilled some of her food. She had been eating apart from the other students and was afraid to ask a classmate to join her. This fear of offending her peers isolated her from the socializing that goes on in school cafeterias and prevented her from making new friends. Her response was to ignore her lack of involvement in social activities and to emphasize her academic achievements instead.

The subject of mainstreaming evoked uncertainty and ambiguous feelings among the rap session participants. Apprehension about competing with nondisabled peers and about academic expectations was evident. Some teenagers felt that they had not received the same kind of education and that they were unprepared to handle the pace of normal classroom assignments. They also had some fears about the reactions of nondisabled students to their disabilities. "My speech is hard to understand; will they make fun of me and think I'm stupid?" "Will they think that I'm too different and be afraid to talk to me?"

Many disabled adults perceive academic standards in special schools and special classrooms as lower than those for nondisabled students. Remembering their own experiences, they feel that their special educations were inferior. They recall having less homework than their nondisabled sisters and brothers and being taught at a much slower pace. Teachers often allowed them to get away with things that would not have been tolerated in regular classrooms. At the time, this leniency may have been welcomed, but most disabled adults regret this differential treatment and the lowered expectations of parents and teachers.

Disabled adolescents have frequently been the recipients of special treatment by family members and other well-meaning adults since the onset of their disabilities. This differential way of dealing with disabled persons stems mainly from the fact that they are viewed as so different that their special needs must be met in special ways. The segregated educational environment, the residential institution, and the sheltered workshop are examples of the special treatment that society affords them. Little consideration is given to the fact that this treatment isolates them from the mainstream of life and prevents them from reaching their full potentials.

Parents and other family members tend to treat disabled adolescents differently from other young people in the family. Relatives may offer special gifts, a special place at the dinner table or family gathering, and immunity from punishment for behavior that otherwise would be unacceptable. Such treatment may embarrass and discomfort the recipient. One disabled teenager admitted that he was given more money than his siblings by his grandparents but then he was put into a corner while they went out to play. "My brothers and sisters couldn't understand why I got ten dollars more or why I couldn't go out and play with them. I felt like saying to my grandparents, 'I'd rather go outside to play than to have an extra ten dollars.'"

Another teenager recalled that during his childhood the special treatment he received aroused feelings of envy and jealousy in his siblings. At times, the preferential treatment isolated him physically, emotionally, and socially. It gave him a distorted view of reality and made it harder for him to develop into a responsible adult.

Some disabled adolescents are treated as if much younger than their actual ages. Adults remember being cast into the role of perennial "kid." Parents who are fearful of leaving a disabled child at home alone often ask a brother or sister to stay with him. This concern can be annoying, but it is much less embarrassing than having your parents hire a babysitter, especially someone who is younger than you are.

All adolescents are sensitive to the treatment they receive from adults. They try to assert their need for a certain amount of independence and self-reliance. Disabled teenagers express these same needs but they have a much harder time trying to satisfy them. Because they are disabled, they are all seen as fragile, vulnerable, immature, and dependent; unfortunately, they tend to assimilate these evaluations into their self-images. "I need help from other people, so how can I expect to have any kind of privacy?" "How can I achieve any measure of independence?" "Will I ever learn to be self-reliant?"

The idea of independent living was discussed several times in our rap sessions. Most of the participants had not given much thought to what they would be doing as adults although they expressed uncertainty about their futures. The idea of independent living and its implications were not very clear to them. Most had only vague ideas about what they might do after high school: "I guess I'll go to college if I can find one that is accessible to people in wheelchairs." "Maybe I'll be able to find a job." They were unaware of the services and financial assistance available to people with disabilities.

Disabled adolescents can never hope to achieve any significant measure of independence or self-reliance unless they are given ample opportunity to develop the skills essential for daily living. Like other teenagers, they need the freedom to experiment, to test themselves and their abilities, to make decisions on their own. The adolescent need for more freedom from parental control is often disregarded when the adolescent is disabled. The efforts of parents, relatives, teachers, counselors, and medical personnel to protect disabled teenagers in fact deprive them of the chance to try, the opportunity to succeed or fail.

The parental urge to protect children from harmful situations is much stronger when the children are disabled. They are seen as more vulnerable and more limited than may actually be the case. Disabled teenagers are discouraged from trying to do things on their own. Limited mobility results in severely limited opportunities to experience many normal activities. Overprotection, which leads to overdependence on others, restricts these opportunities even further. There is no freedom to plan and organize daily activities, make decisions, and solve day-to-day problems. The disabled teenagers may lack ordinary socialization skills. Many disabled adults, including the authors, have had to overcome the effects of overprotection. Many have had to learn independent living skills after reaching adulthood. This task can be very difficult without the benefit of earlier preparation.

For many teenagers, going away to college is a means to achieve more independence. The disabled adults in one rap group had found the experience to be very important because it was their first opportunity to be on their own. It also is the first significant participation in a mainstreaming situation for many disabled students, some of whom may never have participated in any program or activity with non-disabled peers. Sheltered experiences in special schools and special recreational activities cannot prepare anyone to deal with the realities of the ordinary world. Disabled teenagers are often unequipped to manage the academic requirements and competitive atmosphere of the college classroom. They encounter difficulties relating to and socializing with nondisabled students. The problems are compounded by the fact that most nondisabled students and college personnel are equally unprepared for the integration process. They have had little experience with disabled persons and view them with the usual stereotyped perspective that has caused the disabled teenagers difficulties throughout their lives.

Society's expectations for disabled people generally are quite limited, so much so that any achievement is held to be truly extraordinary and success in a field of activity is considered to be the exception to the rule. Parental expectations may reflect the limited view of society or they may be equally unrealistic by imposing much higher goals. Disabled teenagers who are expected to be high achievers face the same disadvantage as their peers who are expected to achieve very little. Frequently, adolescents who are physically disabled are expected to be intellectually superior, perhaps to compensate for their physical limitations. Parental concerns with academic achievement are picked up by the child. Indeed, the parents of one teenager in the rap group stressed her intellectual abilities so much that they completely ignored her social needs, and so did she. She made academic excellence the major focus of her life and did not seem to mind, at least overtly, the lack of friendships with people her own age.

Sometimes, parents base their expectations on what they believe to be normal standards. For example, walking is seen as one way for a disabled child to approach normality; thus, walking becomes an end in itself, with no regard for its efficacy or the toll it exacts upon the mind and body of the disabled child. Some of us have had to endure a great deal of pain and frustration because we were expected to learn how to walk, even if it meant wearing heavy, clumsy braces and resulted in damaging already weakened body tissue. The desire to please our parents was countered by resentment toward the pain and effort walking demanded.

The expectations of others—parents, teachers, and counselors—also influence disabled teenagers' choices of aspirations and goals. If expectations are unreasonably limited, goals will be limited too. But if expectations demand too much of teenagers, they become frustrated and disillusioned. They may find it extremely difficult to select goals for the future; often, they attempt to avoid the whole issue.

In our rap group, the future goals of the teenagers were quite vague. Some wanted to be able to work and live away from their parents but were uncertain about the kinds of jobs they might be able to obtain and how they would live on their own. Parents are often fearful and unsure about their disabled children's futures. Teachers and counselors tend to direct disabled teenagers toward what they consider realistic goals but which are the result, often, of attitudes that label and stereotype individuals. There is an unfortunate tendency, for example, to encourage disabled persons to enter the fields of counseling and social services without much consideration of individual abilities and interests or the realities of the job market. Disabled teenagers need sound academic and vocational guidance based upon their individual abilities and potentials as well as their personal needs and interests. Usually, disabled adolescents have had little exposure to the world of employment and possess little knowledge of the available vocational alternatives.

Mainstreaming disabled students into regular classroom settings will involve some difficulties and will require extra effort from those who take part in the process. Disabled adolescents who have been educated in special settings and have led comparatively sheltered lives outside of school may have academic and social difficulties in the competitive climate of the classroom, in meeting lesson and assignment requirements, and in making friends. Academic performance below the standards of regular classroom students may reflect the lower requirements of the special class rather than lack of ability, however. The attitudes and reactions of nondisabled peers may cause initial interpersonal problems and be heightened by the disabled students' lack of experience with nondisabled populations. Nevertheless, the horizons of both disabled and nondisabled students will be enlarged by the opportunity to learn together and to learn about each other.

# CHAPTER FIVE

# Plunged into the Mainstream

## Stephen Hofmann

In this chapter I want to help educators and other people overcome the barriers of fear that prevent them from interacting with disabled children and teenagers. I want them to understand my frustration about and strong feelings toward what I see happening to disabled children in schools today.

When I was young, I always thought that it would be a big deal to have nondisabled friends other than my brothers and sisters. When I grew up, I found that such friends were very difficult to have. I often had embarrassing experiences because I felt too uncomfortable with nondisabled persons to ask for help. I even thought, at one time, that I had to agree with everything nondisabled friends said if I wanted to keep their friendships. In fact, I played rather dishonest games with both them and myself.

Now, after knowing many nondisabled and disabled persons, I find no substantive difference in my relationships with either. I am living at present with 10 persons, seven of whom are not disabled. We are, in essence, an extended family where everyone is committed to sharing and to doing whatever is necessary to satisfy each other's needs. Disability is not seen as a special issue in our household. To me, this experience suggests a simple truth: that disability can be not only secondary but even inconsequential as a problem. I feel almost bitter when I realize that I and my disabled friends could have enjoyed an optimistic view of our futures all along. We used to expect to be institutionalized upon the deaths of our parents. Much of the present difference in my attitude comes from seeing that I am related to people as ordinarily as anyone else.

To put my views in perspective, an understanding of my personal background and experience is important. At age 15 months I was diagnosed as having cerebral palsy. The characteristics of my disability include involuntary movements of motor muscles and lack of fine motor coordination. I speak with some difficulty but I can be understood. I attended public school in Brooklyn, New York until I was 19 years old. In elementary school I was in a special unit comprising three class-rooms for nine grade levels, several therapy rooms, and administrative offices. The only interactions we disabled children had with our non-disabled peers was in a weekly assembly during which no one was permitted to talk.

While attending Grover Cleveland High School (also in New York City), I had my first opportunity to attend classes with nondisabled students. When I think back, I wonder about the logic of the school system's decision to take me from a totally separate special education environment and plunge me into the mainstream of a regular high school. Did the powers that be think a dramatic psychological adjust-ment would occur during the summer between my graduation from elementary school and my entrance into the competitive high school environment with nondisabled students? When disabled children have been shut out of the regular educational environment for years, they can not be expected to make a comfortable switch into the mainstream without preparation.

After getting through the four years of high school, during which I felt imprisoned, I graduated and went on to Long Island University. Four and one-half years later I received a BS in elementary education from C.W. Post College (LIU did not grant such a degree). I did my student teaching in two public schools, with nondisabled fifth-grade students. After the children's curiosity about cerebral palsy was satis-fied, they accepted me completely. Indeed, the evaluation of my class-room experience noted the "creative discipline" which I had main-tained. Still, the principal never became used to the idea of my being in the building.

Continuing at C.W. Post, I received the MS in guidance and coun-seling two years later. During graduate school I started and ran sup-port services for disabled students to finance my degree. Upon gradu-ation, I moved to California where I have been employed in community services to the disabled and have provided contracted services as an educational consultant.

Under the present laws, students, regardless of the severity of their disabilities, must be educated with their nondisabled peers with the help of appropriate supportive services, except when a child's individual needs dictate another type of placement. The laws, however, have not led to a quick change in attitudes toward disabled children.

Through working with community groups to help parents attain the services needed by their children, I have witnessed much reluctance to obey the mandate, and resentment from school administrations and board members. I become angry when I see another tear rolling down a parent's cheek or hear a parent's voice quiver with emotion at the microphone when he or she addresses board members on the services needed by a child in order for that child to function in an integrated setting.

The combination of counseling and experience in working with children has given me some insights concerning the barriers to changing attitudes about people with disabilities. My main feeling is that most of us, disabled and nondisabled alike, were stifled in important ways when we were young. We were not allowed to stare or to ask questions—prohibitions that created a sense of mystery about and fear of the disabled. Let us now give ourselves the freedom to trust our curiosity.

It is possible for disabled and nondisabled people to have relationships in which a disability merely poses some inconveniences to be overcome. Unfortunately, disabilities are usually viewed as primary characteristics and people's attitudes toward disabilities frequently warp their treatment of the individuals who have them. It is essential that disabled children fall, cry, laugh, and, in general, experience the world without artificial limits. Many disabled adults have learned to close themselves in protective bubbles. We educators must do everything we can to prevent this isolation from happening. I cannot emphasize enough how important and not really difficult it is to attain whatever a disabled child needs to function in school. We are talking about someone to assist the child in, perhaps, reading and writing, walking, eating lunch, or using the bathroom. Even the excretory needs of some disabled young people are not an overwhelming problem when they are dealt with openly and simply.

The experiences acquired in integrated schools with students of varying physical abilities and limitations provide a basic lesson in patience and cooperation. A child's disability can even be used in the curriculum as an educational experience. For instance, suppose the class contains a deaf child and his interpreter; during a unit on foreign languages and why people communicate differently, the deaf child could teach the class the manual alphabet and some simple phrases in American Sign Language. If a child in a wheelchair is in the class, the unit on transportation could be used to take all the children to a public bus stop where they could explore the difficulties of getting onto a limited-access bus.

Teachers can use the natural curiosity of students to help them to get to know their disabled classmates. Occasionally, the pace of the classroom may have to be slowed down to deal with the needs of a disabled child but such instances help nondisabled children to understand their disabled peers. Ultimately, children learn the bulk of what they know from each other. If we, the teachers, can kindle the spark and spirit of warmth, caring, and cooperation among children, we will truly be benefiting all children now and in the future.

### Who Is Disabled?

The label "disabled" is open to much misuse. Although it can be used to refer to people with a specific set of physical or mental limitations, it may provide an undefined label for stereotyping someone different from the speaker. "Disabled" is not generally used as a description of functional limitations, but, rather, as a means of marking off a supposedly distinct kind of person.

Consider, for example, how we never label the victim of a skiing accident "disabled." Such a temporary condition as the inability to climb stairways actually fits the definition of disability but it does not carry the same stigma as a more permanent orthopedic disability.

Actually, every individual has functional limitations. What distinguishes the inability to dress and wipe oneself from the inability to throw a 60-yard pass or lift a heavy weight? Clearly, the technical definition of disability can be applied to the general public. By using the labels "disabled" and "nondisabled," and thereby not seeing a person simply as a person, individuals separate themselves from those who have special limitations. It is true that "disabled" persons may need more of certain kinds of help, but this need should not present a problem beyond that of being sensitive human beings.

### Psychological Fear of Disabled Persons

I would like to explore some of the possible feelings of nondisabled people in establishing relationships with disabled peers. Although the sequence presented gives a clear picture of the feelings that may occur, it is not meant to imply that every individual goes through all the stages in the order in which they are given.

In our society great importance is placed on physical beauty and youth. The epitome of this attitude is found in present-day high schools where one of the major goals of the students is to be accepted; thus, students try to look and dress according to the norm. Even with the proper apparel, however, someone with a disability may find it difficult to be accepted.

People who are influenced by the importance of controlling one's body may find it frightening to interact with a person who lacks that control. The possibility of losing some physical capability that is taken for granted can cause people to want to shut out any individual who displays physical dependency.

If you are "normal," your fear of disabled people probably started when you were very young. Your parents' attitudes had a great bearing on yours, and their uncomfortable feelings about disability probably were conveyed to you. For instance, they may have prevented you either from touching someone who was disabled or from asking questions about the disability. This situation instilled a sense of mystery and fear and introduced embarrassing feelings. Some parents look at disabled people through negative religious stereotypes. In some religions, having a disabled child is a punishment for some sin committed by either the parents or child.

The media also have a powerful impact on the attitudes of the general public, often presenting negative images of disabled people. Until recently, people with disabilities in movies and other media have been portrayed as weak, sickly, ignorant, and not responsible for their own actions. Characters in the popular imagination, such as Tiny Tim (Dickens's *Christmas Carol*) and Quasimodo (Hugo's *Hunchback of Notre Dame*) definitely have an effect on the development of children's attitudes toward the disabled. In recent years, we have seen the proliferation of 24-hour "Telethons" that fill the screen with images of cute but frail and pathetic disabled children. By emphasizing the disability and provoking guilt, pity, and sympathy in the viewers, the sponsors raise large amounts of money. The attitude cost, however, is high. Only through normal everyday interactions with disabled people will the public cease to view disabled people primarily as helpless charitable cases.

Disabled people frequently are considered "ill" and thereby not responsible for their own actions. Although this notion is absurd, healthy "disabled" people often are thought of in this manner.

When children see people with visible disabilities in stores and other public places it is natural for them to ask what is wrong.

All too often the response is "He's sick" or "He's crippled." People avoid contact with disabled persons in insulting ways. For example, an eminent scientist who is confined to a wheelchair travels a great deal with a companion. Waiters will ask the companion, "Does she want another cup of coffee?" as if the scientist is not responsible for her actions and can neither comprehend language nor make decisions.

## Guilt and Pity

Pity toward and guilt about the disabled seem especially strong in some cultures. This seems to be especially true in male-dominated societies. In cultures where a strong emphasis is placed on men being heads of households, physically able to work, and completely in authority, a disabled male who cannot satisfy these requirements may be especially stigmatized. The transference of such attitudes from generation to generation is a very difficult trend to break.

## Ambivalence

Some people prefer not to interact with disabled people at all. The ambivalence created by the fear of disabilities and the feeling of an obligation to be helpful or at least superficially friendly results in apathy. Other people find themselves feeling fearful and wanting to avoid contact with disabled persons, on the one hand, but feeling guilty if they do not provide some help, on the other hand. Such people may make the excuse that the disabled person prefers to "do it himself" or that they don't actually know how to help a person with a particular kind of disability. Generally, such conflicting attitudes create awkwardness for everyone.

The willingness to enter relationships with disabled persons under certain conditions is clearly shown by some people. They may feel comfortable with disabled persons in their homes or in some kind of residential setting but they would be embarrassed to be seen with the disabled persons in public. For example, a young man might feel comfortable with a disabled girl when they were alone but in public he would be upset over how other people would perceive the relationship. Or a nondisabled person might get along fine with a disabled peer until the latter needs some physical assistance; then the nondisabled person may resent having to provide the help. Sometimes, nondisabled people interact successfully with disabled persons in groups but pull back from more personal, one-to-one relationships.

## Awareness

People who are disabled are as diverse as the nondisabled population. They can be warm, loving, gentle people who care a great deal about other human beings or they can be selfish, conniving, manipulative, and self-centered. A major key to awareness is to react to a disabled person in the same way that you would to anybody else.

Imagine that a disabled student gets into trouble for violating a school regulation that carries the punishment of an automatic five-day suspension. What action should be taken? In fairness, the punishment should not be negotiated because the student is disabled; parents should not be called unless that is regular school procedure; and the student should be suspended for five days.

Homework is an essential learning task. While writing this chapter I was having a very difficult time because all my teachers used to pat me on the head and say, "You're doing great! Keep up the good work!" instead of demanding more effort from me and supporting my writing. We love kids; we are proud of them; and we get impatient with them. Let us, however, hold these strong feelings for all children, disabled or nondisabled.

A wheelchair is only a chair with wheels, but in this society many stigmata are attached to it and to any kind of orthopedic appliance or alternative learning equipment. When people are able to recognize that wheelchairs can be smashed or that orthopedic appliances are merely objects of metal and bolts that mean neither sickness nor lack of responsibility for one's actions, we will break a major attitudinal barrier toward disability. One way for teachers to help dispel this barrier would be to borrow from a surgical supply store a wheelchair, cane, and walker for a day for the children to play with. By allowing them to freely explore the devices a sense of familiarity and acceptance will emerge.

### Toward Awareness

In this chapter I have tried to pinpoint some of the feelings that may be barriers to initiating relationships between disabled and nondisabled children. The important point to remember is that these feelings are not unusual but that most people feel embarrassed about sharing them. As an orthopedically disabled adult writing from my own perspective on life, I would like to make it clear that only openness and honesty from the entire school community, from children through board members, can make mainstreaming work.

Many laws protect minorities from being educated in segregated settings. The laws that apply to disabled students are just as important to implement as those dealing with racial desegregation. When we talk about the integration of disabled students, basically, we are talking about having a down-to-earth educational process by which children, regardless of the severity of their disabilities, can be fed, wiped, walked, or pushed. In addition, we must stop robbing nondisabled students of the experience of playing and learning with disabled students; otherwise, we are not preparing them for the future world where disabled and nondisabled persons will work together.

School board members should remember this goal when making crucial fiscal decisions for funding supportive services to enable all disabled children to go to their local neighborhood schools. Administrators should remember this objective when they are developing, implementing, and monitoring programs for essential supportive services to disabled children. Teachers should keep this end in mind when writing their lesson plans and developing Individual Educational Programs (IEP's) for their disabled students. Parents of disabled children should remember this goal before signing their child's IEP to make sure that the child will receive all the supportive services he or she needs in order to have the optimal positive learning experience.

Parents must also remember that they make up the backbone of their child's equal opportunity to receive the "least restrictive, free and appropriate education." They must never be intimidated by school personnel. They must trust their own intuition and knowledge that comes from being with and helping their child all the time. At all times, close communication should be maintained between special education resource personnel, parents, disabled students, and classroom teachers.

This chapter is meant to help the reader to begin a new learning experience. I hope that it has defused many of the misconceptions and fears that have arisen around the presence of disabled children in schools with their brothers and sisters, and that it has placed the focus, above all, on having fun with all children and letting all children have fun with their strengths, their weaknesses, and their creativity.

Parts of this chapter may have been uncomfortable to read; I hope, however, that having suffered through the discomfort, readers will feel a great deal more comfortable about relating to disabled children, teenagers, and adults.

I would like to end with the thought that if I, as a child, had gone to school with you, there would have been no need for me to write this chapter.

# CHAPTER SIX

# Loss of Hearing: Coping with a New Reality

## Zannet Coleman

**M**y hearing began to decline gradually at age 12½, just as I was completing sixth grade. At first I refused to believe I was anything less than a perfect human being with total use of all my senses. It was an insult to me if someone described me as deaf. I was quick to register my protest and have the remark corrected. "Oh, she can't hear." This statement I could cope with more easily.

The first three years, during which I made the transition from "hearing" to "not being able to hear" to being "deaf" were the hardest. I actually went through three stages of personal change, from disbelief to fear and depression and finally acceptance. I had a long silent battle within myself that no one knew about.

As my hearing loss increased, my speech became impaired. Much of my ability to communicate and understand others was dependent on my above-average ability to lipread. In many conversations, when I could respond correctly and intelligently, I had a difficult time convincing others that I "couldn't hear" or that I was "deaf." Most people were in awe or taken aback that they were actually speaking with a deaf person. These situations were sometimes dramatic, sometimes comical, and at times sad.

My last few weeks in sixth grade, just before I was medically declared "becoming deaf," were really difficult. I was suffering a gradual decline in hearing. My lack of ability to pick up information in group discussions in a class of 30 to 40 students was becoming frustrating. My teacher would call on me to lead a class discussion and I couldn't handle it. "Zannet, can't you speak up louder?" "Zannett, can't you hear what I said?" "Zannet, can't you speak more clearly?" In the past, I had always been an active participant in class activities. But now my participation began to decline, with much disappointment and frustration for me and my teacher. I knew he was wondering what was going on. In truth, I think I was frightened. I really didn't know what to make of it. I couldn't believe I was actually becoming deaf. Ridiculous! How another 12-year-old would have handled the situation, I don't know. But when the truth was finally inevitable, it was hard to accept, incredibly tragic and sad.

### Social Relationships

Because of my deafness there were obvious attitude changes among my peers. A lot of them just couldn't cope with the fact that I was deaf, or going deaf. I couldn't talk on the phone anymore. On summer nights I stopped playing my favorite neighborhood game of hide and seek because it was just too dark and I couldn't lipread.

Some of the kids I knew began to make fun of my speech, too. I didn't sound the same anymore. I can remember them asking each other, "What did she say?" "I don't know!" Giggles. I would crumble inside, I was so ashamed and hurt. I found a solution to all this. I just stopped associating with most of my peers. I began to withdraw. I took all this inner agony with me into books. I'd shut myself up in my bedroom and read. I only spoke when spoken to. I stopped being open with people. I just read and read. I would read so much that my mother would get angry and take away my books. At night she would have to force me to turn out the light. On occasion, I would read with a flashlight under the covers.

This situation got so bad that my mother had to consult a doctor for advice. He felt that this withdrawal was only leading me on a road to personal disaster. So I was put on a strict schedule. I had a time limit on reading silently, and had to read aloud for 15 minutes each day. I was forced to play outdoors more. I was encouraged and persuaded to do everything a normal child would do at that age. In truth, I was treated as if there had been no change in me.

### Public School Struggles

I attended seventh grade at a public junior high school, where I experienced a damaging defeat to my personal self-esteem—removal from the fast learner, "bright kids" class. Everything went wrong. The teacher was new to the school, and he was a rapid lecturer with very little movement. Exams were given orally and answers were to be written within a specified time limit. The teacher never repeated anything twice and had very little patience. No matter how hard I tried, I couldn't lipread him. I couldn't follow without the help of visual aids, and he considered me an impediment to the progress of the class. I was transferred to a slower class. Of course I was hurt. Somehow it didn't diminish my positive attitude toward learning, but I didn't have too much admiration for that teacher.

Now 13 years old, I was the only deaf child in the entire junior high. My new teacher went out of her way to make me feel welcome by *everyone* in the class. I was placed in the front row at her favorite location in the room. She had eyes like a hawk, and I can recall her saying so often, "Zannet, you must pay attention so you can read my lips." I understood everything she said because she cared and took time to be repetitive and to use visual aids.

Even though I felt I was a favorite, I didn't experience any resentment from my fellow classmates. I was often used as an example for others to follow because I was quick to learn and completed assignments with a minimum of errors. I seemed to fit into that class perfectly. I kept contact with this teacher for many years. She is one of the many people who made an impression on me and motivated me to do my best. Little did I or my parents realize, however, that I wasn't learning what I should have been. Gradually I began falling further behind, losing time on the education that was rightfully mine.

Eighth grade was a breeze! Much of the class routine was the same. The only differences were that I had a male teacher this time, and that I missed more than a third of the school year because of major surgery which kept me hospitalized for more than a month. People thought I was dying—I was so sick. I also had a spinal injection and they didn't put me to sleep—oh! That was murder! I had to learn to walk all over again, and couldn't participate in physical education classes. I also received speech therapy at a local medical clinic for about 6 months. I took speech and lipreading when all the other kids were having P.E. and music.

In hopes of helping me "get my hearing back," my mother quit her nursing job for two years to take me to doctors all over the area, trying to find out what was happening to me. She tried everything. It was heartbreaking to both parents that I failed to improve. But I did graduate with my junior high school class of 400 in the spring of 1963. I was delighted that they didn't keep me back.

### Developing Social Confidence

Because of my age at the time of my hearing loss, many of my social experiences were in a coeducational context, and always chaperoned.

More often than not, I was the only hearing impaired individual in the group. I grew up in an integrated environment, where Black youngsters, like me, were well accepted. There were picnics, parties, swimming, baseball games, bowling, and rollerskating events. By the time I reached high school, through the end of my first year in college, I had developed a particular interest in one young man who wasn't hearing impaired. We got along tremendously. He was the only person with whom I felt free to share my inner feelings about my fears and the tribulations of being disabled. He could always lighten the depressive moods I experienced. He was also very protective of our relationship. Many of his peers, particularly the girls, would tease him about "running around with a deaf girl." But peer pressure only increased our determination to stay together, which we did. This relationship helped me maintain confidence in my ability to associate with my hearing peers and enjoy it. The experience was a fundamental contribution to my self-trust and self-esteem.

### Residential School: A New Experience

A major milestone in my life was my enrollment that fall in the state's residential program for the deaf. I was angry and rebellious toward my mother in particular. I didn't understand why I couldn't attend high school locally. I was angry because I would be forced to live away from home and could only see my friends on weekends. I would be forced to accept my disability openly, and I still hadn't done that within myself. I would be forced to live with other deaf kids and I was afraid. I had no idea what to expect, and no previous association with other deaf persons. I didn't know anything about sign language. Although I was terrified, I was secretive about my feelings.

I did take a brief tour of the residential school before being accepted. I was upset that the administration had decided to put me back in the eighth grade. The people testing me felt that I couldn't handle anything beyond this level. I was given some basic arithmetic sheets to do, and I did them in a flash, but this still didn't change my placement. I was aware of the examiner's surprise, however, and knew I had made a good impression. Since then, I have discovered that a large number of students accepted at that school are not considered very intelligent. Eighth grade subject matter was more like fourth grade work in a public school.

My first encounter with almost the entire student body of the high school was during lunch period on my first day on campus. Remember, I didn't have any idea what to expect in this special school. When I entered the main dining hall, which looked to me like a large dome-shaped hangar where airplanes are constructed, all I could see were bodies seated from wall to wall with arms weaving back and forth in the air. Precisely at that moment, all I could think was that I had entered a completely foreign land. "What in the world am I doing here?" I was just thunderstruck and at a loss for words. So I simply stared.

I even remember getting into an argument with a student over the salt shaker. Using speech, I asked someone to pass the salt, please. No one responded to my request. Finally, I became visibly angry, which attracted the attention of the other students at the table. Before I knew it, there I was yelling, saying all sorts of things, and there they were, making all kinds of facial expressions, moving arms and fingers. Neither of us understood the other. They couldn't lipread and I didn't know the slightest thing about sign language! It was very frustrating.

My new teachers were good to me, and because of this I was able to transfer out of the eighth grade in a few weeks. The work was too easy. I remained in ninth grade until midyear, and then moved on to the tenth grade level. I met my match in the class of 14 pupils—12 girls and two boys. My teacher was demanding, and he wouldn't accept anything but the student's best efforts. We *had* to prepare ourselves as if each upcoming class were a midterm exam.

Our teacher made sure we never lost contact with the outside world. We had daily assignments in current events and political happenings around the world. Like clockwork, we had quizzes on these events. We were taught speed reading, Latin, politics, poetry, and we went through all the classical novels that most hearing kids study in public schools. Each day, at the beginning of class, we stood with our heads bowed in a minute of silence to think about the less fortunate people in the world. With this teacher, you could *never* do too much work. It was prepare, prepare, prepare for the future—no exceptions.

I always felt that this teacher had a very optimistic attitude toward his students. In his opinion, being deaf or handicapped was no excuse for not being able to master higher educational goals. His teaching methods paid off in later years. It was his determination and our sweat that laid the foundation for all of us to enter and complete a college education.

I did experience envy from some students once my tenth grade placement became permanent. I was 14 years old in a sophomore class whose enrollment included some students who were over 20 years old. I had been a healthy, hearing child for the first 12 years of my life, while most of my classmates had either been deaf since birth or had experienced their hearing loss at a very early age. They didn't accept me, and it was easy to understand their resentment at having someone so young placed on their level. For a time there was some rivalry.

During the previous two years, I had experienced periods of disbelief, withdrawal, and depression. Why me? Why be born with perfect hearing and then become deaf for reasons no one would ever know or understand? When I finally found peace with myself in the residential school, I began to love the place and considered myself fortunate to be a part of the educational system.

Where else would a young deaf teenager be encouraged to mature, to grow in leadership skills, to devote time and determination to drama, to go all out in athletics, to understand politics and the techniques of organizing a meeting and following Robert's Rules of Order? Where else would someone like me learn more about deafness, relate to other deaf individuals, and learn to cope with and overcome obstacles to learning and self-improvement?

Some people criticize the institutional setting that has the deaf individual spending a major part of the growing up years in a residential school, allowing the school to carry the major responsibilities of upbringing. It's true that living away from home does have an impact on families and the child involved. But every child has a right to be educated. Living away from home does not remove parental authority. Parents have every right to be kept fully informed concerning their child's activities. Parents need to be involved in the educational system as much as their child needs individualized instruction and special education.

The doors to learning on our campus were open to all students of all racial and cultural groups. There was a total school involvement, a positive atmosphere, and unity among the students, whether they were poor or well-to-do, White or Black. This is the impression I learned to live with and the experience which planted the seeds of my philosophy of living.

### On to College

My first year at Gallaudet College was a challenging one, as I learned to live independently, make my own decisions, and balance my time between work, play, and rest. There was so much freedom at college compared to the secondary level residential atmosphere, where students were supervised and had activities planned for them daily. Like many of my peers, I was largely unprepared for the new experiences awaiting me in college. It took a lot of determination to make it through. Most did. Others left because of financial difficulties or the inability to maintain passing grades. The opportunity to have a good time and forget our essential purpose at college was always hanging over us.

### Reflections on the Black Experience

It would have been nice if ethnic studies had been a part of the school curriculum during the time I was a student at the residential school for the hearing impaired. What little was said about Blacks was what appeared in our American history books. I didn't learn about Black culture until my junior and senior year of college. Those Blacks who were affiliated with the state residential school worked in food services, the janitorial department, grounds department, or security. Only one was a teacher, and a handful were clerical workers. It's a shame to say this, but I never had a Black teacher in my life.

In college, there was a small group of Black students that numbered about 20 out of a total school enrollment of 800 to 1,000 Whites and foreign students. Males outnumbered females 2 to 1. Two among our small group were from California, several from D.C., others from Florida, South Carolina, New York, Mississippi, Atlanta, Chicago, and African nations.

Although we had identity problems, personality flair-ups, occasional jealousies, and a struggle for leadership within the group, the fact remains that we were all proud and considered ourselves special to be the only Blacks on campus. Most of us could talk; some even had hearing. If there were any racial issues or resentments I experienced, they occurred here, among this small group of 20. We were forever criticizing each other for being an Uncle Tom, for not living up to our Black heritage, for dressing better or worse than one another, or for being materialistic. This rivalry existed more among the females than among the males. However, deep down within each of us there was a sense of unity and loyalty in being the only Black deaf persons pursuing a college education at that time. This unique experience helped me understand other Black deaf individuals of different backgrounds who had a less fortunate life than my own and who, unlike me, had to struggle financially to make it through college.

### Employment: An Uneasy Transition

My parents never felt it was necessary for me to work or get a job before finishing school. During my senior year I did seek odd jobs, with the assistance of the placement department of the college. Not until I had graduated from college did I experience the problem of unemployment for the handicapped. For about a year, I looked for a job. Newspapers were devastating. Ads for office positions or clerk typists always specified some telephone responsibilities as being essential to handling the job. I wasn't accepted. The results of my efforts fell into one of three categories: (1) phone work I couldn't do because I was deaf; (2) being told I was overqualified because of my college degree; (3) a promise to contact me as soon as my application was screened, which of course never happened.

If I had no difficulty communicating with a prospective employer, I wouldn't mention my deafness until later in the interview. As soon as my disability became known, a very negative attitude surfaced. People would try to appear nice and sympathetic, but this attitude was all artificial and an affront to me. This is the impression I got. It was frustrating to experience this on a first-hand basis. It made me realize what an extra hard time I would have in finding a job, if I ever did! For a while I was depressed, and I felt that my college degree wasn't worth the time and expense it had taken to achieve it. I found it easy to understand why many deaf individuals who have little language are unemployed and on welfare, and how being Black, deaf, illiterate and poor must be one of the worst situations imaginable.

# CHAPTER SEVEN

# The Deaf: Handicapped by Public Ignorance

## Leo M. Jacobs

Admittedly, this narrative is more personal than professional. I am writing it from the point of view of a person who has been deaf all his life and who has been a professional in the educational field for more than 40 years. As one who has experienced the daily frustrations and irritations caused by deafness, my point of view differs markedly from that of a hearing person who writes about deafness only vicariously. If such persons were able to experience deafness subjectively, some of their theories might take a different cast.

Before discussing attitudinal patterns, a short historical perspective on deafness is in order. During this country's early years, nothing was done for its deaf citizens; they were left in limbo, uneducated and dependent upon others for life support. Had it not been for some good persons who were concerned about the problems of deafness, deaf Americans might have remained in this dependent status much longer. Thanks to Thomas H. Gallaudet, Samuel Gridley Howe, Laurent Clerc (a deaf teacher from France), and others, most of us have been able to obtain the education needed to become self-supporting adults. This education, however, was not necessarily superior.

The first efforts to educate deaf persons were made solely by hearing educators. They established educational policies from a vantage point that was entirely outside the realm of deaf people's experiences. They had only external contacts with deaf persons to guide their course of action. They did not, and could not, obtain any inkling of the deaf individual's intrinsic problems.

As a result of looking at deafness from a purely outside viewpoint, hearing educators became most concerned about making the deaf individual as nearly "normal" as possible. Thinking that the only way to live was to be hearing like themselves, they focused on instilling in the deaf the expressive communication skill of speech and the receptive skill of lipreading because the disability blocks the channel of sound. Little did they realize that a person must know what he or she is talking about before uttering the first sentence.

In recent years I have had the opportunity of working and interacting with orthopedically handicapped individuals. I found a parallel in the outside community's attitude toward these special people. They complain that the able public seems concerned with their performing like normal persons—that is, being able to walk. So they are pressured into using leg braces, canes, or crutches; the wheelchair is used only when all else fails. Even when settled in the chairs, they are still under pressure to use those which must be manually steered so they will stay in better physical condition by exercising their upper bodies. Many paraplegics are much more anxious that their wheelchairs be dependable and easy to use; they are interested in quick repair service and motorized chairs. In addition, they are concerned about the availability and quality of attendants. Obviously, they are more accepting of their disability than their able friends and, therefore, more concerned about improving the quality of their way of life.

So it is with deaf people. They want to be able to communicate in a more relaxed and comfortable manner than they are able to if limited to oral communication, which is imperfect and elliptical, and requires a great deal of guessing and improvising by deaf individuals. They are also more interested in the quality of their interpreters; they want to be sure that messages from the hearing community are clear and unambiguous and messages to that community are read and interpreted correctly.

The traditional methods of educating deaf children, however, were to teach them to speak even before they had an opportunity to comprehend their environment and to deal with it. A few talented deaf children would make the headlines along with their proud benefactors. Unfortunately, the great majority of children failed to get an adequate education through this purely oral method. Subsequently, they became inadequate deaf adults. Many deaf persons cheated as children by using home-made gestures secretly. Woe to them if they were ever caught using those awkward gestures! Spanking, having their hands tied, being tied to chairs, and other barbaric measures were used to discourage manual communication.

I was one of the fortunate few deaf children who had deaf parents and who grew up with Ameslan (American Sign Language). Thus, I experienced no deprivation in communication. It was difficult for me to comprehend that the horror stories told by my deaf friends actually could have happened, although I occasionally came upon similar situations when I visited oral classrooms on my errands. I would see perspiring, exasperated teachers shake deaf children, and put them out in the hall or in a corner for using their hands in talking, or clutch students' chins to force them to stare directly at their teachers in order to learn proper pronunciation.

In those years, educational programs were usually administered by hearing adults, who foisted their theories upon a deaf populace that was mostly pliable and uncomprehending of what was happening to them. The deaf were not only unaware of their rights as consumers of those educational practices but they were also unaware that much better avenues of communication existed. The hearing educators practiced rampant paternalism, disregarding any deaf person who dared to question their policies or theories. Manual communication was held in low esteem because, theoretically, only oral "failures" used it. (Little did those hearing teachers realize the extent to which deaf adults used sign language once they got out of the hearing professionals' sphere of influence!) Unfortunately, hearing parents and the hearing public subscribed to the same attitude toward manual communication.

I have two daughters, one who is hearing and one who is deaf. Naturally, we used manual communication at home and both of our girls are adept at it, having grown up with it. My wife and I decided to send Lisa, our deaf daughter, to the local day school program for deaf children which was then strictly oral. We found most parents obsessed with having their children achieve near-perfect oral skills. As deaf parents, it was an ordeal for us to attend the PTA potluck dinners at the school. When we entered the room we could almost feel the freezing atmosphere descend upon us. Every time my wife and I tried to carry on a dialogue, using manual communication, we felt disapproving eyes boring into us. No one attempted to make us feel at home at all.

Later on, during our daughter's last years at the day school, the total communication philosophy began to be accepted. The attitude of the other parents toward us became more cordial. Once a mother even decorated a cake with hands spelling "Hi." Strange to say, the PTA soon became weak and ineffectual, probably because it no longer had a cause to champion.

For over 150 years the deaf community encountered a climate of disapprobation every time it brought out in the open its primary means of communication. McKay (1969) has described the climate in his article on the dynamics of minority groups.

It was probably the militancy of the Black minority which finally led the way for other disadvantaged minorities to come out in the open and express their frustrations and dissatisfactions. Finally, the public is being awakened and sensitized by the deaf themselves, rather than by paternalistic hearing professionals.

Although the National Association of the Deaf (NAD) has been the chief voice for deaf consumers since 1880, it was not until recently that the NAD came out of the closet to become an influential organization and a protagonist for deaf citizens. As the public became aware, so did the government it supports. With the help of the government, deaf citizens have gradually won respect for their own language and public attitudinal support for their right of self-determination.

Although the position of the deaf in America has never been as good as it is now, we still have a long road to travel before we can hope to become first-class citizens, on the same level as hearing citizens.

One problem is the residue from inappropriate educational programs. Many deaf adults in the country are in great need of effective social services. Although counseling and referral agencies for deaf adults are appearing everywhere, they are only beginning to scratch the surface. The scope of services provided by existing agencies needs to be greatly expanded and more agencies need to be added. Many deaf citizens have additional handicaps, which multiply their needs and frustrations. These additional problems can be physical or of ethnic origin.

A good example is the experience of Black deaf citizens. Schools for the deaf in the South were traditionally segregated; Black schools were usually inferior. These schools have been desegregated and are undergoing the transitional period very well. I think deaf youngsters are less prejudiced than their hearing counterparts, probably because of their disassociation from their own society. This alienation leads to a delayed awareness among deaf youngsters of what is going on in their neighborhoods or communities, including manifestations of prejudice.

Another problem is the implementation of Public Law 94-142, which provides for the mainstreaming of disabled youngsters in public schools. The passage of this law caused concern rather than excitement among knowledgeable professionals in the field of deafness. Rapid and effective communication is one of the basic ingredients for the successful integration of special children into regular classrooms. Deaf children make up one of the very few groups of disabled children who are likely to be unable to handle this situation. Communication, even through competent interpreters, is usually only about 75% effective. Good interpreters are in short supply; when the schools settle for less than top quality interpreting services, deaf children suffer even more isolation and deprivation. The very nature of the interpreting situation causes deaf youngsters to lag in the educational process. Obviously, it is very difficult, if not impossible, for the deaf to participate spontaneously in class discussions.

Deaf teenagers find it difficult to interact with their hearing peers outside the classroom. Without teachers or older leaders who can continually supervise and motivate integregation, the process is likely to break down after some abortive efforts by the hearing children to include their deaf peers in their activities, simply because effective communication cannot be carried on continuously.

P.L. 94-142 provides for special facilities for handicapped children when they are necessary. However, the provision of special services may instill a sense of failure in these children. This situation is frequent among deaf children, who may carry within themselves a sense of failure all their lives, especially if they come from disappointed hearing families. If deaf students are successful in being mainstreamed, they will probably be a small minority that is different from the student body as a whole. This may contribute to a haunting feeling of inferiority among hearing-impaired students.

What happens to deaf youngsters who are "isolated" in special facilities? There follows an excerpt from a brochure issued by Gallaudet College, the only liberal arts college for the deaf in the world. The excerpt is also applicable to secondary education programs because, during these stages of development, outside activities assume an important role in the growth process of young people.

Q. Would not a program for deaf students on a hearing college campus be a more nearly normal situation?

A. A "normal" situation is one in which students communicate freely, work and study together as they wish, participate in a full range of college activities, and develop their own life style and social affiliations. Life on Kendall Green [Gallaudet College] is more nearly "normal" for a deaf college student than his life would be on any college campus for hearing students. At Gallaudet College students have opportunities to participate in sports, fraternities and sororities, student body government, drama, and professional and academic organizations, developing thereby a wide range of social and leadership skills. Some deaf students can and do succeed academically in colleges or universities primarily for the hearing. More often than not, however, a deaf student on a hearing campus is "odd man out." He is often a social isolate and cannot develop and exercise his non-academic skills.[1]

There is a growing interest among hearing Americans in learning the third most used language in the country—sign language. It is a pleasure to continually come across waiters, clerks and other persons

---

[1]The brochure, *Plain talk about Gallaudet College*, is available from the Director of Admissions, Kendall Green, Washington, DC 20002.

who are able to use sign language. At the same time, progress has been slow in providing deaf people with interpreters so that we can inter-mingle completely with the general community. This problem can be-come a life or death matter in medical or courtroom situations.

The federal government has been foremost in solving this problem by funding the training and certification of interpreters. However, it will be a long time before we can interact with our environment readily and easily, either through interpreters or with those hearing citizens who have learned our language.

The adages, "Communication is the soul of the community," and "Communication is the key to mental health," may be platitudes but nothing can be truer in the case of the deaf person. Even a slight impediment in the flow of communication immediately sets the hearing-impaired person apart from the everyday stream of the hearing world.

After years of being the victims of faulty communication with family and school personnel, with subsequent misunderstanding and frustrations, young deaf adults are usually happy and anxious to join the society of their own kind. With them, the young adult can throw off the shackles of halting communication and become a fully participating member of the deaf community where communication is free and easy. This fact has been difficult for the hearing friends of deaf persons to accept.

A well-known hard-of-hearing principal of a Midwestern school for the deaf finally got tired of attending meetings where hearing adminis-trators continually discussed their concerns about integrating deaf chil-dren into the hearing society. He broke into such a discussion to ask, "What's so great about the hearing society?" It would have been amus-ing to see the dumbfounded expressions of the hearing persons!

The question is probably the best illustration of how most deaf adults feel: They do not have the slightest desire to integrate into the hearing community, not only because communication is difficult and frustrating, but because deaf culture is very attractive. They can de-velop a sense of belonging only when they are with their own kind; they know that they would be only lookers-on at the fringe of a hearing community, not in the middle of activities as they are in the deaf society.

I do not mean to imply that deaf persons are unable to be self-sufficient in the hearing society. With few exceptions they have proved to be excellent and dependable workers. They and their hearing co-workers have developed special systems of communication; there have been few instances of deaf workers being let go solely because of their inability to get along with and interact with their fellow workers and supervisors. Indeed, in many cases the inability to hear has meant that they are subject to fewer distractions and are more likely to give full and continued concentration to their work. More often than not it is due to preconceived stereotypes and prejudices of supervisors that deaf people fail to achieve upward mobility, rather than to lack of qualifications.

Thus, most of us successfully support ourselves and our families, own homes, drive cars, do our errands, and behave just like the hearing; therefore we are noticed by strangers who pass us on the roads and sidewalks. Indeed, we do not feel that we are really disabled and it is difficult for us to identify with other physically disabled groups. The inability to communicate with our milieu is more of a nuisance than a real handicap to us. I would think that hearing persons could experience comparable situations if they visited places where few or none of the inhabitants spoke English.

Hearing citizens may "discover" deafness when they attempt to communicate with us, much to their dismay and frequently, irritation. Deafness is so invisible that the average hearing person, unfamiliar with this disability, finds it difficult to comprehend how extensively it affects us. The crippling effect of deafness takes place in ways that are not readily seen and therefore the implications of deafness are not easy to identify. Because of this fact deafness usually gets a lower priority than other disabilities which are more visible and discussed more. We are probably handicapped most by public ignorance. This ignorance is also manifested by many other disabled citizens with whom we frequently have to compete for public dollars.

An excellent example of this ignorance was evident when I attended an all-day workshop conducted for disabled consumers by the Metropolitan Transportation Commission in Berkeley. Representatives of the various transit systems around the bay area were invited to exchange information and concerns with the disabled participants. All day the discussion centered around the "transbus," which would accommodate patrons in wheelchairs. Almost nothing was said about the needs of the blind, the deaf, and other categories of the disabled. From a panel of the transit personnel we found out that every transit system had a task force committee composed of disabled consumers; when I questioned the panel it became evident that only one task force had a deaf member.

At noon we were all asked to leave the room while the tables were set for lunch. On our return, we found that only half the tables in the room had been set and our table was one of those not set. So, we four deaf participants and interpreters attempted to find places together elsewhere; however, other participants quickly took places and held empty places for their friends. We ended up standing around when everybody else was seated because only a few single scattered places were left. Finally, places were set at one of the vacant tables so we could sit together.

At an afternoon panel, I reviewed what had happened that day to demonstrate that deaf people were usually ignored and given the last priority, even by other disabled groups. It was then that several of the other participants apologized profusely for their actions at lunch, and I was beseiged by the transit people to submit names of deaf citizens for participation on their task forces.

Deaf awareness efforts are continually being made so we can hope that the public as a whole will become fully aware and sensitized to deafness, its problems, and its needs. When that day comes, American deaf citizens will know that they have gained their rightful place in society.

## References

Jacobs, L.M. *A deaf adult speaks out.* Washington DC: Gallaudet College Press, 1974.

McKay, V., & Makowsky, B. Deafness and minority group dynamics. *The Deaf American*, 1969, *21*, 3–6.

## Recommended Reading

Bowe, F., & Sternberg, M. *I'm deaf too: 12 deaf Americans.* Silver Spring MD: National Association of the Deaf, 1973.

Brill, R.G. The Superior I.Q.'s of deaf children of deaf parents. In *The California Palms.* Riverside CA: School for the Deaf, 1969.

Holcomb, R.K. *Hazards of deafness.* Northridge CA: Joyce Media, 1977.

Katz, L., Mathis, S., & Merril, E.C. *The deaf child in public schools—A handbook for parents.* Washington DC: Gallaudet College Press, 1974.

Kohl, H.R. *Language and education of the deaf.* New York: Policy Study #1, Center for Urban Education.

Mindel, E.D., & McCay, V. *They grow in silence.* Silver Spring MD: National Association of the Deaf, 1971.

Mow, S. How do you dance without music? In J.A. Little (Ed.), *Answers.* Santa Fe: New Mexico School for the Deaf, 1970.

# CHAPTER EIGHT

# Blindness: Disability or Nuisance

## Kenneth Jernigan

People who become blind face two major problems: (a) They must learn the skills and techniques that will enable them to carry on as normal, productive citizens in the community and (b) they must become aware of and learn to cope with public attitudes and misconceptions about blindness—attitudes and misconceptions that go to the very root of our culture and permeate every aspect of social behavior and thinking.

The first problem is far easier to solve than the second. It is no longer theory but established fact that with proper training and opportunity the *average* blind person can do the *average* job in the *average* place of business, and do it as well as his or her sighted neighbor. The blind are functioning today as scientists, farmers, electricians, factory workers, and skilled technicians. They are performing as housewives, lawyers, teachers, or laborers. The skills of independent mobility and communication and the activities of daily living are known, available, and can be acquired. Likewise, the achievement of vocational competence poses no insurmountable barrier.

Despite the availability of alternative techniques and the established fact of the capability of blind persons, the blind are seldom offered training that leads to independence; if they are given such training they are rarely permitted to exercise their independence.

The real problem of blindness is not the blindness itself—not the lack of sight or the acquisition of skills, techniques, or competence. The real problem is the lack of understanding and the misconceptions that exist. These misconceptions go back to the days when a blind person could not dodge a spear. In today's society, dodging a spear is not an essential ability but the stereotype of helplessness has remained intact, surrounded by a host of other stereotypes: The blind are simple, spiritual, musical; they have a special sixth sense; their other senses are more acute—in short, they are different and apart from the rest of society.

In fact, the blind are largely isolated from society, although this isolation is ending rapidly. The relative rarity of blindness (two in 1,000 are blind) means that most people will seldom see or know a blind person and will rely on the stereotypes found in literature or on television. Beyond this, blind people have suffered from a tradition of work with the blind that emphasizes custody rather than integration. Many blind persons do not work in private industry but in special sheltered workshops. The work is often the same as that done in industry (except that the equipment in workshops is often outdated and the pay scales are far, far lower) but the blind are there because rehabilitation counselors and private employers cannot imagine them doing any other work. Many more blind persons, of course, work neither in private industry nor in workshops. Public attitudes force them to spend their lives sitting at home in idleness. According to a 1972 study, 70% of the employable blind are either unemployed or work only a few hours a month at menial jobs.

The attitudes of society toward blind persons permeate not only the media and literature but, also, the minds of professionals who work with the blind and of the blind themselves. If we are to change these attitudes, certain questions must be addressed first: How are these attitudes expressed? What is their effect on blind persons? How can they be overcome? What sort of programs for the blind are best able to produce independent, participating citizens?

My observations are based on several areas of experience. I am myself blind and have been since birth. For the last 30 years I have been part of the National Federation of the Blind, the largest organization of blind people; the Federation's membership now includes 10 per cent of the blind population. For the past 10 years I have been the elected president of the Federation; and for the past 20 years (until 1979) I directed the Iowa state agency for the blind, where the programs were based on the philosophy set forth here and where our success has been nationally and even internationally recognized.

In discussing public attitudes, let me begin with an example that shows how seemingly innocent stereotypes produce crippling results. I speak of the lovable cartoon character Mr. Magoo. Because he is almost blind he bumbles and blunders through a series of bloopers—walking into telephone poles and apologizing to them because he thinks they are people, patting the tops of fire plugs and speaking to them as children, and walking up half-finished skyscrapers. The humor is based on the exaggeration of the stereotype; the public believes that blindness is somewhat like this but the overstatement is meant to remove it from the realm of cruel mockery.

What is the effect? Some time ago a blind woman from Indiana called me. She said, "The other day I was at the home of a friend, who is also blind; and her four-year-old son was watching Mr. Magoo on television. He turned to his mother in hurt and bewilderment and said, 'Mother, why are they making fun of you?'" My caller went on to tell me that later that same week she was walking down the street when a small child spit at her and said, "You're old Mr. Magoo." The woman was so shaken by the two incidents coming together that she called to ask what the Federation could do about it.

Let me take the example further. During 1974–75, an agency in the Northwest, Community Services for the Blind, made Mr. Magoo the center of a fund-raising campaign. When the Federation protested, the sighted president of the agency wrote, "The advertising message is especially directed at people who are *responsible* for the blind—not the blind themselves. We don't feel the blind person will tend to identify himself with Mr. Magoo necessarily; in fact, many may not even know who he is . . . . If there is any kind of a negative aspect in the fact that Mr. Magoo has poor eyesight, it is all the more effective, just as a crippled child on a muscular dystrophy poster is more effective than a normal child."

This response indicates a good deal of what is lacking in many agencies that provide services to the blind. There is the notion that someone must be "responsible" for the blind. There is ignorance of the effect such negative publicity has on the blind. There is the disregard of the contributions of blind people themselves. Finally, we should note that the response defends the use of Mr. Magoo—an admittedly false image of blindness—on the ground that it will be more *effective*. Two statistics put this latter point in perspective: (a) According to a 1976 Gallup poll, Americans fear only cancer more than blindness and (b) the American public contributes many millions of dollars a year to various charities dealing with blindness.

We have barely scratched the surface of the public's images of blindness, however. Some of the examples I give might be disregarded as being based on the lowest level of social awareness; however, they indicate underlying cultural assumptions. Other examples show how these degraded assumptions are dressed up and put forward as enlightened sociological advances.

A blind woman in Ohio wrote:

> During a cab ride on Sunday, I learned to my consternation that the cab driver had always assumed that blind girls, as he put it, "got fixed by doctors so that they would have nothing to worry

about in that way." I didn't feel equal to inquiring whether the problem was that blind girls couldn't handle the emotion or the children. I set him straight, but I learned that you never know when you will meet extraordinary ideas.

It only remains to add that in a number of Eastern states, there are blind people alive today who were sterilized by the state.

Even when it is not expressed so brutally, this stereotype is going strong. A blind couple, who had an 8-year-old daughter of their own, applied to adopt a Vietnamese orphan. The husband holds degrees in social work and supervises teachers in the New York City school system. They were turned down, however, because "It would not be fair to the child to deprive her of parents who could see, and all that means."

A woman in Connecticut wrote:

The other day, when I was picked up for my class in transactional analysis, the priest whom we also picked up inquired of the minister who was driving the car, "What clinic are we taking her to?" He automatically assumed that I must be a charity case, and he was astonished to find that I was one of his colleagues in the class.

A dental hygiene student in California wrote to me:

I am working on a research paper concerning the special needs of visually handicapped or blind people with regard to dental care. I hope to determine: (1) how the dental procedure needs to be altered to accommodate them, and (2) special dental problems of these patients.

Another researcher wrote asking about the special needs of blind persons about to be married; he was studying the training techniques they would need for the wedding night! If he had read a 1973 article in the *National Enquirier* (Nov. 11, 1973) he might not have bothered. The article was titled "Finds Blindness Upsets Sexual Functioning" and began, "The sex drives of the blind are upset by their inability to see light, states a West German researcher."

An expert on penology and social reform wrote to me to say that, in his opinion, the blind (regardless of their misdeeds) should not be put in the penitentiary. "If the seriousness of their offense merits incarceration," he wrote, "they should be dealt with in a special manner." This absurd notion can be contrasted to a decision of a parole board some years ago that although a blind prisoner was eligible for parole according to usual standards, he should not be paroled because he was blind. Or compare it to the letter sent to me by a teacher:

I can find no criminal statistics in the Annual Uniform Crime Report in which blind people are a part. I have assumed for 25 years that blind people cannot become criminals due to this sight limitation. I teach a course in the correction and prevention of delinquency and crime, [and] a 26-year investigation of criminal phenomena has confirmed the Bible's statement that, "if ye were blind ye should have no sin."

By way of answer, I sent him a newspaper headlined, "Blind Man Kills Landlady."

A New Orleans newspaper featured the headline "Blind Children Hate Food, Must Be Force Fed." The article quoted a staff member of a Louisiana institution for the blind as saying, "A blind child would starve to death if you didn't force him to eat ... they hate food." (New Orleans *Times-Picayune*, September 1975).

Ironically, the stereotypes about blindness are often most intense not in the public press or the minds of the general public but in the literature prepared specifically for people who work with the blind. The professional literature on blindness abounds with techniques and concepts that derive from and reinforce the age-old stereotype of blindness as helplessness and inability. Federal statutes guaranteeing basic civil rights to the handicapped have been widely interpreted by agencies and schools to mean that special and separate facilities must be created for the blind. Thus we read (in the *New York Times*):

The first apartment building in New York City designed for the exclusive use of the blind will be built on a vacant site on West Twenty-third Street, officials of the Associated Blind, Inc., said yesterday. The nonprofit group is planning a 12-story structure with 205 apartments. It will include textured doorknobs so that each resident will know which room he is entering, an emergency call system in each apartment connected to a central security office, and specially designed kitchens and bathrooms.... The apartments will be designed in accordance with new national HUD standards for the blind and handicapped. (April 7, 1977, p. 1.)

A special kitchen for the blind designed by students at the Illinois Institute of Technology with the advice of several well-known agencies for the blind included the following features: a rest area to "combat fatigue," work areas with different textures and raised edges "to provide clues for identification of reference points," floors with varied textures "to give blind people awareness of location," electrical outlets with large metal plates at waist level for "ease of locating," and many,

many more. It only remains to add that blind persons need none of the special adaptations recommended for these apartments and kitchens; indeed, when I read these descriptions to an audience of blind persons, they were reduced to hysterical laughter.

What is difficult to convey is the cumulative effect of these stereo-typed attitudes. They are all-pervasive in the experience of blind people; they make up the context of the society in which we live. Nothing can convey this as well as a letter I received from a sighted woman who was dating a blind man. The woman is a special education teacher and the man works for the federal government. She wrote, in part, as follows:

In my experience I have come in contact with the "pitying reaction" ("Poor pitiful little thing; it must be awful to go through life like that"); the "brave and wonderful syndrome" (everything the child does is somehow beyond the realm of human expectations— "My, aren't you smart!"—the child is always described as special and brave; nobody expects him to be able to do anything, and when he does, praise is grossly out of proportion); and "rejection" (the child is ignored or avoided).

Jim and I have experienced a mixture of all three. Friday night, Jim and I had some people over for a cookout. I was in the kitchen fixing baked beans and deviled eggs. Jim came in and asked if there was something he could do. I asked him to slice the tomatoes. (I never meant to start a riot. I only wanted the stupid tomatoes cut up.) One of the other men came in the kitchen and said, "But he might cut his finger." Jim told him that he had cut tomatoes before and was sure he could do it again. He did so and soon had a nice plateful. The other man, who stayed to watch, then took Jim by one arm and the plate of tomatoes in the other to show everybody what he had done. (A cerebral palsied child who has just learned to walk doesn't get that much praise.)

Jim then proceeded to walk out back and light the charcoal. The same man said, "Are you going to let him do that?" I shrugged and said, "Why not?" The man jumped up and ran out back. When he came back, all he could talk about was how re-markable Jim was.

Everyone calmed down and we began to eat. Then it started to rain. Jim got up and said to me, "Are the car windows down?" They were, so Jim proceeded to run outside to roll them up— without his cane. The other man jumped up and grabbed Jim's cane. He said, "Does Jim need this?" I said, "No. Don't worry so about him. He's fine." Jim came back and we started to eat again. Jim wanted some more beans, so he went to the stove and got them. The comment then was, "That is just wonderful." What is so wonderful about dipping beans? Jim told me later (after they had left) that he felt like taking a bow after everything he had done. I don't think he did anything out of the ordinary, and neither does he. The whole night he felt as if he were on exhibit, and I was experiencing a strong desire to stand up and scream, "He's not stupid, and he's not a child. He's not doing anything terrific, so shut up!"

It didn't end there. Later on that night, Jim and I made a trip to the hospital emergency room. He had got into some poison ivy and it had spread to his eyes. The nurse on duty was horrible. She didn't think he was remarkable—she thought him to be blind, deaf, mute, stupid, and incapable of doing anything. She asked me, "What is his name? Where does he live? Do his eyes itch?" I was offended and said, "I think he can answer his own questions." Jim calmly told her what she wanted to know, but I could tell he was mad.

When he went in for treatment, a man came over to me and said, "You are so wonderful to be kind to that poor man." I tried to explain that I felt lucky to have a man like Jim. After I finished trying to explain to this man our relationship, he said, "You mean you're dating him? Why would a pretty little thing like you want him? He's blind." Then I said something I should not have said, "Yes, he is blind, but he's more of a man than you'll ever be." Jim came out of treatment then, and we left.

Saturday afternoon some more friends came over, and we all went roller skating. It was fun and we all had a good time. When we got back to Jim's apartment, one of the girls said to me, "You really are good to Jim. He needs somebody like you." I told her that I needed him, too. She then asked me if when we were alone he was able to do all the things that other men do. You can imagine my shock at such a question. I assured her that he was.

By Sunday, I was so overwhelmed with all that had happened I couldn't think. Jim knew something was wrong. I told him that I was okay. He had some cans that needed to be labeled, so I started doing that on his brailler. I was putting a label on a can of pineapple juice. I spelled it wrong. Jim said he had never seen it written that way. So I cried. He looked utterly shocked that I was crying over pineapple juice. So he said, "I'm going to ask you one time what's wrong, and if you don't want to tell me, that's okay; but I'd like to be able to help you with it!" So I told him.

I told him that I didn't think it was fair, and that I loved him too much to watch him put up with all that mess. Jim is a sweet, loving, compassionate, intelligent, sexy, desirable man; I love him, and it hurts for everybody else to treat him like some kind of freak. He's got such a good self-image. And I don't want that changed. He said, "Honey, take it easy. You'll get used to it." No, I won't. I am not going to get used to seeing him insulted.

I just can't understand what difference it makes whether he sees or not. One of our friends recently said to me, "You really are an exceptional person that you can accept Jim." I said that I really wasn't, and that I just didn't think about it. She said, "Oh, it must be hard to forget a thing like that." I told her that I didn't try to *forget* it, I just didn't *think* about it—the same as you don't think about the fact that someone has brown hair. It really makes very little difference what color his hair is, and it's the same way with Jim. I know he can't see, and I don't try to forget about it, but I don't really think about it. She couldn't understand.

The experiences related in this letter are those of every blind person. To put it simply, the experience of being blind is dominated not by the lack of sight but by the negative attitudes of the sighted public. These attitudes are universal, whether they are overt—as in the case of the child who spat at a blind woman and called her Mr. Magoo—or hidden behind a wall of abstract theories and jargon. And the attitudes are mistaken—they are false. The woman who wrote to me compared blindness to hair color. Most people would reject that comparison. But the blind people who have gained appropriate training, who have overcome the artificial barriers created by misunderstanding, and who have been given a chance to hold regular jobs and lead normal lives, know that blindness can be reduced to the level of a nuisance.

What this means is that the blind are a minority, in the same way that Blacks or Jews are a minority. Their condition is not so much limiting as it is unpopular. The restrictions and denials of basic freedoms experienced by the blind are motivated by good intentions, but the result is discrimination.

The disparity between the reality of blindness and the accepted image of it has become greater as alternative techniques have improved and as our society has depended less and less on dodging spears. By the late 1930's, the disparity had become obvious to many blind people. They began to recognize that their problems were imposed by society rather than by nature. In 1940, blind persons from across the country formed the National Federation of the Blind. This was a recognition that, scattered and few in numbers and in wealth, the blind could only combat negative attitudes through raising a united voice that would express their own experiences and needs, rather than relying on their traditional custodians to do it for them.

The Federation's concepts of blindness are those expressed in this chapter. They have now been accepted broadly in the field of work with the blind, as well as in services for other disabilities, and in the state and federal programs and civil rights laws for the handicapped. The successes have been obvious, but the enormity of the task still to be completed is no less obvious. The examples used here all occurred during the past few years. Still, there is no question that the blind today are closer to acceptance and full integration than at any other point in history.

One measure of the progress of the blind as a minority group is, ironically enough, a more overt resistance to their shedding of the traditional blind person's roles. This has occurred at two levels. The first, and much less important, has been resistance from some professionals in the field of work with the blind. Regrettably there are still people who enter work with the blind because they cannot be dominant in their homes or social or business lives; they feel (whether they verbalize it or not) that at least they can dominate and patronize the blind. This urge often expresses itself in charitable works and dedicated sincerity, which does not mitigate its unhealthy nature or make it any less inappropriate. Twenty—even 10—years ago, this was a major obstacle to the advancement of the blind. Today it is dying away.

In its place has emerged a more subtle but far more pervasive sort of backlash—a backlash that, by its appearance, has validated the concept of the blind as an emerging minority. Here is what I mean by a backlash: When I became director of Iowa's programs for the blind in 1958, the problems were difficult but they were of a different nature from those facing the blind today. A building had to be found for the Commission for the Blind; a staff had to be assembled and trained; and blind persons had to be encouraged to gain self-confidence and belief; they needed instruction in skills and techniques. The governor, the legislature, and the general public had to be persuaded to provide the money and support to make the programs possible.

Difficult problems, but essentially noncontroversial. On the surface there was no violation of traditional notions about extending a helping hand to the blind and the fact that the blind needed that helping hand. In those days (almost 20 years ago) it was not uncommon for passers-by to watch with tears in their eyes as blind persons learned to use their canes to cross streets and move independently through busy traffic. So the program was launched in an atmosphere of general acclaim.

Then, something started happening. Trained for full participation in community life, the blind began to seek it, talking not just about gratitude but also about their rights as citizens. They called denial of equal consideration for jobs discrimination; they asked to receive insurance on equal terms with others unless it could be shown that they were a greater risk, and the state insurance commissioner agreed and issued the rule. They asked for equal rights in the rental and purchase of housing, attendance at educational institutions, use of public transportation, and access to all public accommodations available to others.

These demands are the source of the problem. This new role of the blind is taking some getting used to on the part of the public. Some of the very insurance companies and landlords and employers, who supported the training programs that led inevitably to the present insistence of the blind that they be allowed full participation, are now resenting the results. In effect they are saying, "The blind are getting too pushy. They should stay in their place."

There is no such thing as a free lunch; the blind will have to pay for the new freedom they seek. They will have to be willing to assume responsibilities as well as rights. They will have to give up the security of being taken care of and the countless little privileges which they have enjoyed.

The public, too, will have to give up some of its cherished traditions—the pleasure of treating the blind like pets and children instead of equal members of the community—and its feelings of superiority.

The blind of today have, almost to a person, made their choice of these alternatives: they choose full lives and integration into society. The public, once it understands the alternatives, will also choose to accept the blind as neighbors and colleagues, as equal citizens. They might as well. The blind have already tasted full participation and they are saying, "We know who we are, and we will never go back."

# CHAPTER NINE

# Parents and Professionals: Irrational Assumptions in Their Communications

Bobby G. Greer
Barbara Galtelli

Ideally, the liaison between parents and professionals should be the strongest link in the chain of services provided for disabled children. However, interactions between parents and professionals are frequently distorted by communication difficulties. Certain assumptions, held by one or both participants, may cause these difficulties. Some of the assumptions actually represent the basis for and manifestation of more global attitudes. For example, if one party in an interaction assumes, consciously or unconsciously, that the other party is being untruthful, all communications between the two will be unproductive. Thus, if we want to initiate changes in the attitudes of parents and professionals in order to make communication between them more effective, it is essential that we examine some of their irrational assumptions.

Assumptions are manifested in many ways. The most obvious is in the words exchanged. Other more subtle forms, sometimes difficult to pinpoint, may exist in the realm of nonverbal communication, that is, in tone of voice, gestures, eye movements, and body posture. (For studies of the effects of the more subtle nonverbal behaviors that communicate attitudes, see Davis, 1973; Knapp, 1972.) This chapter examines some of the irrational assumptions which prove most destructive to productive communication; the focus is on how these assumptions impede parent-professional relationships.

It must be pointed out here that not every one of the irrational professional assumptions is held by every professional; likewise, not every irrational parental assumption is held by every parent. Nevertheless, enough of these assumptions are operating enough of the time with both parties to weaken the professional-parent liaison. Neither professional nor parent will consciously admit to an irrational assumption because expressing it openly may make its absurdity obvious. The irrational assumptions held by parents are somewhat developmental in nature in that certain assumptions operate at different times, depending on the frequency and length of contact with professional personnel.

The terms "professional" and "parent" are used in the general sense in this chapter. The first includes all persons who deliver some service to children in a professional role, such as special education teachers, regular classroom teachers, administrators, physicians, and therapists. The second includes all persons who fulfill the parental role for children, such as parents, guardians, grandparents, and other relatives or surrogates.

### Irrational Assumptions of Professionals

*I know a great deal about the limitations a particular handicapping condition will place upon a child.* This assumption has many irrational bases. First, our present-day knowledge of the causes and effects of and, most important, remedial procedures for any condition with which we deal may be negligible. Second, the extent of our predictions about the restrictions imposed by any handicap on any child is more limited than our knowledge of the conditions themselves. Some children progress beyond anyone's expectations, some children regress for no apparent reason, and most children show some improvement. Why? We really do not know. We may suspect that a certain treatment based on a particular theory was the reason for the improvement shown by a child but then we are faced with the fact that other children are progressing just as well although they received a treatment based on an opposing theory. Nor do we know why two children with the same limitations progress differently with the identical intervention. We can speculate on the reasons: individual differences, poor parenting, and motivation; but validating such speculations is not yet within our capabilities.

Many parents, including the authors, have been told that their children would progress only so far and no further, but time proved the "prophets" to be wrong. Sometimes, professional forecasts for a child have a happy ending; that is, the child progresses much further than the professionals predicted; at other times, the predictions have been overly optimistic. Most professionals exercise caution in forecasting but some show less discretion in order to "bring parents down to earth" or to "prepare them for the worst."

*I am not emotionally involved, therefore I can be more objective.* If any professional working in the field of special education is not somewhat emotionally involved, perhaps he or she should seriously consider a change of career. A more subtle form of involvement is exhibited by some teachers, administrators, teacher trainers, and, alas, researchers who are "emotionally involved" with theories, dogmas, and other prejudices upon which their actions are based. Try telling a behavior-management enthusiast that task analysis is useless in a practical setting like the home. Does he react as he would if you told him, "The weatherman said there is a 20% chance of showers today"? No. He will probably react with more intensity. Or try telling a reading specialist who supports the phonetic approach that the "look-say" method is better for some children.

As professionals, we may not be directly emotionally involved with a child and/or family; however, when it comes to what we consider right for the child's progress, we, like the parents and other concerned persons, are very much involved emotionally. I have observed many professionals make very harsh, critical judgments on how a parent views and/or interacts with a child (e.g., "Mrs. W. is overprotective"), as if the claim that they are not emotionally involved in some manner validates their observations.

*Parents do not see the "big picture"; thus, their priorities for their children sometimes are not appropriate.* Can we be sure the professional sees the "big picture"? What is big to one person may not necessarily have the same dimensions for another. More important, the parent normally spends more time with the child than does the professional. What the child can or cannot do at home may be more important and strategic to the parent. The child's abilities or disabilities in day-to-day tasks around the home have a definite impact on the parent's routine. For a child to be able to partially feed himself at mealtimes may not be so important to the professional but it may be the ultimate concern of the parent. Both parent and child would benefit if the professional took seriously the "realness" of parental concerns. If professionals were of tangible assistance to parents in aiding their household routines, then they would do more to promote positive attitudes in parents than through counseling.

It also should be obvious that professionals know the sequence of teaching skills, generally. Certain skills must be mastered before other more meaningful skills are attempted. However, it should never be assumed that such sequencing is obvious to parents. It is the teacher's or therapist's duty to apprise the parents of such factors. Too often, however, informing parents of the specific details of intervention methods which may be used with their children are felt to be above the parents' heads. For example, one of the authors and his wife were told that their daughter needed surgery before she could properly articulate sounds because of a cleft palate condition, but the surgeon kept saying that there was "no rush." Not until they had a multidisciplinary work-up on the child by a third, independent facility were they informed that early surgery might be neutralized at puberty with the elongation of the facial bone structure. Had they been given this information earlier, they would have been better able to make decisions regarding alternatives for their child.

*The manifestation of parental hopes, aspirations, and dreams for their children indicates the lack of acceptance of children's limitations.* Handicapping conditions, by their very nature, place varying degrees and kinds of limitations on children. Yet the specific limitations imposed by any disability on any child are difficult to ascertain. We should ask ourselves, therefore, if it is morally right for professionals to place too much emphasis on the negative aspects of a child's limitations. Should we dash a parent's hopes in order to prevent "unrealistic" expectations? Do we ourselves know what constitutes "acceptance" of people in general and disabled persons in particular? Unless we can answer such questions affirmatively and unequivocally, what moral right do we have to judge others?

One of the authors was once in an intensive training program studying the multidisciplinary approach to the treatment of cerebral palsy. One session involved a parents' group meeting. At the conclusion, a parent invited members of the group to come live in his home for a short period to observe what life with a severely impaired child was like. Subsequently, a professor interpreted the parent's invitation as an attempt to rationalize his rejection of his child by proving how miserable life with such a child was. The author, having had some extended experience in round-the-clock management of several youngsters with different handicaps, still does not understand how the professor could have so interpreted the parent's invitation.

From a humanistic point of view, we can say that all persons survive, to varying degrees, on hope. Some hopes are reality based, others are not. But the significance of hope is not in whether it is reality based, but in whether it provides an existential reason for being. Do we do parents justice by dashing such hopes, whether realistic or not? Certainly, all of us have encountered extreme examples of parental expectations which have had adverse effects on children. But should we generalize these extremes to *all* parents? On the other hand, there is some reason to believe that many limitations on the behaviors of handicapped children actually are imposed by the educational system and society. Hence, we might do better to focus our efforts on reducing and/or removing those imperfections in education and society that limit children rather than dwelling on the intrinsically limiting factors of handicaps.

The preceding irrational assumptions are a few of those which the authors have observed in themselves and other professionals. Several more could be added to the list, of course, but these four appear to operate more frequently and more insidiously than others. The point, however, is that it would be well for professionals to take stock of the irrational assumptions upon which their attitudes and behaviors are based.

### Irrational Assumptions of Parents

Basically, parents' assumptions can be classified into two categories: (a) those about professionals and (b) those about their disabled children. The assumptions in both categories may be present or absent or may vary depending upon the extent of the parents' interactions with professionals.

### Assumptions About Professionals

*Professionals are wise, well educated, and all-knowing in regard to my child and his condition.* Professionals and parents alike may wonder what is irrational about this assumption. Other than the obvious limitations on our knowledge of any child's condition, a more subtle irrationality is present. First, this assumption usually is held by parents who are rather naive about what and how much professionals know. Such parents have had little interaction with persons trained to work with disabilities. Typically, the parents are so eager for answers and assistance that they may be reluctant to offer information which they have about the child if it contradicts what they think the professional is saying. For example, the professional may express the opinion that the child has a "learning disability," and go on to state that many children with learning disabilities are hyperactive. Although, in fact, the child may have no hyperactivity problem, the parents may conjure up instances to support the alleged hyperactivity rather than to appear to argue with the professional. Such parents often confuse being polite with total submissiveness; they assume that the professional's opinion is right because he or she is a professional and that their common sense and observations cannot be trusted. When parents withhold accurate information, it is wrong to damn the professional for forming a wrong opinion. The following abbreviated case history is illustrative.

*At the age of 6, Roy had been referred for testing because he reversed numbers and letters. The school psychometrist administered a Bender Gestalt, Wide Range Achievement Test, and Peabody Picture Vocabulary Test on the basis of which Roy was removed from the first-grade class and placed in a special education learning disability classroom. The parents accepted what they were told by the professionals and Roy stayed in the special class doing motor exercises until mainstreaming came into effect. The parents were then told that it would be socially beneficial to put Roy back into the regular classroom and to provide him with tutoring in academics in a resource room. The resource room teacher found no signs of reversal or inversion, only a child who had not been taught academics. At the end of one year, Roy could read on a beginning third-grade level and work corresponding math problems. The psychological report on reevaluation stated that the learning disability program had cured Roy and made him ready for academics. The parents were as accepting of this report as of the initial diagnosis and everyone was happy except Roy; he was fighting to catch up on everything he had missed. At no time did his parents ever question any decision relating to him.*

In other instances, parents do not understand the terminology used by professionals. In attempting to cooperate with administrators, psychologists, and teachers, such parents may misinterpret what was asked or said. Not wanting to appear ignorant or stupid, they answer queries or agree with statements that actually may be contrary to the facts. These instances are basically examples of parents going along with professional opinion because of reluctance to refute or argue with professionals.

When parents have had extended encounters with professionals they sometimes develop, accurately or inaccurately, opposition to professionals and their role.

*Professionals, by and large, are stupid, arrogant, and pompous.* Unfortunately, many parents, whether they admit it or not, hold this assumption to some degree, whether out of intimidation, frustration, or valid and humiliating encounters. Such a blanket indictment of the professionals charged with assisting children to overcome their limitations is unproductive to say the least. Not all the "blame" here lies with the parent, however. Because of the behavior of some professionals, there is a degree of substance to this irrational generalization. However, the issue is not fault or blame but better communications for the benefit of the child.

The best way to enhance professional-parent communications is to look at these assumptions for what they are, and to eradicate them as far as possible. Parents must not fall into the trap of trying to prove the professional wrong for their own satisfaction; this endeavor may salve their egos but it does little to assist their children. Likewise, professionals should examine their behaviors and try to correct those that may tend to support this assumption. Do they make dogmatic statements? Do they adhere to positions to "save face" when they know such positions can not be defended?

Finally, after lengthy encounters with professionals, some parents come to adopt more positive assumptions.

*Professionals have a job to do and do not really care about the child as an individual.* This assumption is, perhaps, the saddest end to which professional-parent interactions can come. Despite previous experiences, parents should not write off professionals as uncaring any more than they would want someone to write off their children as hopeless. Professionals, as a group, do care. They may appear callous for a number of reasons: fatigue, fear of their limitations, or any number of other problems and feelings. In many cases, unfortunately, the fact is that these very professionals have cared too much and have experienced their own disappointments. The assumption is not the reason for the behavior at issue but it functions to impede communications. Too many parents take such a position; through their behavior they "program" professionals to be uncaring.

Parents, like professionals, should examine their own thinking. Do they make the foregoing assumptions about some professionals? In what respects do their thinking and/or behavior reflect the assumptions? We advocate group counseling with parents regarding their children's problems. Now, we may consider advocating group sessions with professionals and parents that will focus not on the children's problems but on the professional-parent relationship itself. Both parties might learn a great deal about themselves.

Someone once said, "Respect is the product of respect." Not until parents and professionals air their assumptions about each other can respect in such relationship be reestablished and progress occur.

Teachers, particularly, at the middle school and secondary levels, tend to give parents the impression of not caring. The fact that a professional may be tired, fearful, or *afraid* to care too much does not excuse the appearance of callousness. A professional is identified by the ability to override emotions and carry out responsibilities. If that responsibility deals with handicapped individuals, a professional who *appears* to be uncaring is not being very professional.

### Assumptions About Children

*My child's condition, situation, or problem is unique and cannot possibly be fully comprehended by any professional.* The fact of individual differences gives an obvious grain of validity to this assumption. However, it often functions counterproductively in the professional-parent relationship. If a parent holds strictly to this assumption, he or she may write off any and all recommendations made by professionals who lack total empathy. All of us, at times, rationalize our failures to adhere to advice or rules because we must deal with a "different set of circumstances." "Yes," we say, "that may be true as a general rule but ... " At some point, parents must learn to concede that their children's situations are not unique, that some methodologies, strategies, and interventions which have proven effective for other children may be effective for theirs if given half a chance. It is possible that parents hold on to this assumption in order to prevent the build-up of hope which may be crushed by the failure of an attempted treatment or intervention. The following case history is an extreme example of the counterproductive nature of this assumption.

*Joseph was diagnosed as mentally retarded with autistic tendencies and placed in a class for autistic children. He had no spontaneous language but was echolalic. His mother fought with everyone. She refused to acknowledge that Joseph was retarded. According to her, "He has a slight communication problem. He should be in the regular classroom." She got him removed from the autistic class and put in a class for emotionally disturbed children; then she demanded that he be excused from the teacher's requirements for the class because he was "not like those other children; he is different. He needs a program specifically designed for him. He can read anything." She refused to accept the educational diagnostician's report that he was a "word caller" and did not understand what he was saying. She constantly denied that he totally lacked spontaneous language, stating that he demonstrated expressive language at home and that it was the fault of the psychologist and the school system that he did not perform anywhere else. Who has the biggest problem, Joseph or his mother?*

*I (the parent) have overlooked "something" which might have benefited my child greatly had I only known.* In many respects, this assumption appears to be diametrically opposed to the preceding one. However, it must be remembered that the assumptions we are discussing here are unconscious and largely irrational; thus, opposite assumptions can be held side by side.

Of all parental assumptions discussed so far, this one may be the most destructive. It gives rise to chronic feelings of guilt. To entertain the idea that one could have done something which would have reduced and/or prevented the seriousness of a child's condition is most painful for parents. Yet, almost every parent of an exceptional child has had these feelings on one or more occasions. Also, few "sage importations of advice" will put this belief to rest. There may have been something which could have been done which would have alleviated the child's current condition. This statement represents ineffective hindsight, however. The child's future not his or her past should be the focus of concern. The authors know of no particular method or strategy that is effective in dealing with this assumption, with the exception of stressing future plans for the child.

*Dale's mother blames herself that he has been labeled "learning disabled." She smoked two packs of cigarettes a day while she was pregnant and feels that the habit caused his problems. Because she feels so strongly about her possible contribution to his condition, she inevitably does the one thing that compounds Dale's difficulty! She excuses his inappropriate behaviors—both social and academic—and hovers protectively over him. She agrees that he needs structure and needs to be taught to be responsible for his own actions, but every time a situation occurs in which she should "bite the bullet," she cannot do it. It is her fault that he has this problem to begin with—isn't it?*

*To expect too much improvement in the child's present condition is unrealistic and a sign of "lack of acceptance" of the child.* Unfortunately, when this assumption is held by parents it is reinforced through their interactions with friends, family, and, particularly, certain professional personnel. Like the assumption on the "omnipotence" of professionals, this one assumes that current prognostications for a child are firmly rooted in a base of valid data. This is not the case. Many unknowns will influence a particular child's circumstances. If the foregoing is correct, then how can the lack of realism be defined? There are extreme examples, of course. However, 20 years ago, it would have been extremely unrealistic for a parent or anyone to expect that many nonvocal children would have the aid of a device like the Auto-Com (an electronic communication aid for nonvocal children). New developments in technology occur daily.

The essence of the nonproductivity of this assumption is the feeling engendered within the parent that *hope = lack of acceptance* and *lack of acceptance = rejection* of the child. Can we say a person rejects reality and the world as it is if that person hopes for world peace? Too often, however, we find ourselves labeling as "unrealistic" the hopes of parents concerning their children; thus we set in motion the foregoing "cognitive-emotive" equations. Actually, a case can be and often is made for the opposite statement: lack of hope is a sign of resignation and rejection of the child. Therefore, it seems that we subliminally expect a parent to walk a very fine line between too much unrealistic hope and dismal stoicism. Who is actually being unrealistic?

*Sally has cerebral palsy. She is nonverbal and the most severely involved child we have ever seen. Her teacher told the mother that Sally was hopelessly retarded and would never learn. Even if she were not retarded, there was no way to test or teach her. The mother was advised to institutionalize her. Sally sat in the first-grade classroom for one year and no one worked with her. At the end of the year, after her mother had complained all the way from the principal to the school board, it appeared that Sally had learned nothing. In desperation, her mother enrolled her in a demonstration school at a university. At the end of two weeks, Sally—using a pointer—demonstrated that she could indeed learn to read and had in fact absorbed some instruction during that miserable first year in school. Because her mother refused to give up, by age 11 Sally had developed communication through a specially designed electronic device and had made a trip to Washington to "talk with" the Secretary of HEW. Although once classified as hopelessly retarded, she has demonstrated above-average intelligence and a sparkling personality, and she has provided considerable insight into how to test and teach nonverbal children.*

*Parents are actually responsible for how their child "turns out," that is, for what the child becomes.* This particular irrational assumption is not restricted to parents. All of us have been swayed, to some degree, by the line of thinking that the environment is the major factor determining the intelligence, motivation, learning achievement, and emotional make-up of a child. Recently, substantial evidence has emerged that the environment, and parents in particular, may not be as influential as was once thought. We do not wish to resurrect here the nature versus nurture controversy, nor to speak specifically of the influence of the environment on the child's learning ability. What we are attempting to convey is the fact that despite apparent optimal environmental conditions, things frequently go awry. Conversely, despite the most malevolent environment, some children develop most adequately. The point is that our overemphasis on the role of the environment has sent many parents on a "guilt trip." They feel responsible for things that do or do not happen to their offspring.

In the long-term progress of the individual, development is influenced by a number of factors outside the power of parents to control. Constitutional make-up, biorhythmic factors, nutritional considerations, the influence of the media, and other such elements frequently have a definite impact on a child's development, but parents exercise only limited control or power over them. Too often, professionals, with their almost childlike faith in the popular theories regarding the critical roles of parent and environment, advise parents of their responsibility for childrearing duties; the ultimate assumption is that the child is what you make of him or her. It is becoming increasingly evident that things are not this simple!

## Summary and Implications

We have attempted to review some nonproductive assumptions which are held by professionals and parents in relation to the special child. The assumptions reviewed are held to be irrational and, thus, to interfere in the establishment and maintenance of rapport between professional and parent. For the most part, such assumptions operate on an unconscious level and are manifested in diverse, subtle ways. We have alluded to some behaviors by professionals or parents which can be taken to be outward manifestations of such assumptions. However, there are many other ways, not noted here, in which such assumptions surface behaviorally. We hold that most irrational assumptions are largely manifested in subtle nonverbal behaviors. In a much larger sense, attitudes of all types are most clearly seen in the study of nonverbal communications. Research and demonstration projects are vitally needed in this area not only to pinpoint specific behaviors impeding rapport and communication but, also, to identify ways of changing such behaviors and their underlying attitudes. That is the next frontier for attitudinal research.

## References

Davis, F. *Inside intuition: What we know about non-verbal communication.* New York, McGraw-Hill, 1973.

Knapp, M. *Non-verbal communication in human interaction.* New York: Holt, Rinehart, & Winston, 1972.

# CHAPTER TEN

# Parents, Practices, and Attitudes: The Distance Traveled

## Kathryn A. (Gorham) Morton

O ne of my current professional responsibilities—my favorite—is supervising a small, specialized collection of books, journals, and newsletters for parents of children with mental, emotional, and physical handicaps. The library has 1,000 books, most published within the past few years. I find it disheartening to be unable to keep up with the influx of literature for and by parents but it is a happy complaint. Eighteen years ago, when I was just beginning the struggle to understand the *what's* and *why's* of having given birth to a retarded child, the writings of parents in comparable situations were scarce on the shelves of the public library. There was an armful of publications at most: Pearl Buck's *The Child Who Never Grew*, Dale Evans's *Angel Unaware*, Dorothy Murray's *This is Stevie's Story*, Marie Killelea's *Karen*, and a few others. I recently reread *The Child Who Never Grew* (1950), one of the earliest personal accounts by a parent of a retarded child.

Buck describes how she bore "the sorrow of having such a child." She narrates her search for a place where her daughter would be "secure for life" and described the private institution she found where the motto, "Happiness first and all else follows," hung above the director's desk. He talked to her "gently and gravely," telling her,

> You must remember that these are happy children. They are safe here. They will never know distress or want. They will never know struggle or defeat, nor will sorrow ever touch them. No

demands are made upon them which they cannot meet. The joys which they can appreciate they have. Your child will escape all suffering. Will you remember that and let it be a comfort to you? (Buck, 1950, p. 47)

By contrast, the literature of the late 1970's by some parents and all professionals is filled with quite the opposite message. It documents very clearly the need to challenge children, to let them incur risks, to let them, above all, be an integral part of the mainstream of community living and learning. One of the strongest opponents to segregated special education is lawyer Tom Gilhool. In a paper presented in early 1978 to a workshop sponsored by the Bureau of Education for the Handicapped, he laid out a careful argument for outlawing not only institutions but also special schools. He suggested integrating all children into regular schools, his strategy for ending discrimination. He analyzed the "least restrictive environment" criterion of Public Law 94-142 as follows:

Analysis of the meaning of the statutes shows that certain settings are generally impermissible under the law, e.g., segregated special education centers and institutions.... Thus implementation and enforcement can focus, e.g., on the necessity of moving self-contained special classes to school settings where non-handicapped children are being educated. (Gilhool, 1978, p. 4)

We have come a long way. In the mid-1960's I was strongly advised by every professional I met to put my very severely retarded daughter in an institution for the same reasons that were given to Pearl Buck 15 years before that. In the 1970's we rescued children from back wards and taught many of them to walk, talk, feed, dress, and toilet themselves. Now, under the "least restrictive imperative" of the law, we have come a full 180 degrees; *all* children are to be educated in regular schools, near, if not with, their nondisabled peers.

How did we come so far? What happened in between? How did it feel to parents? The literature of the 1960's and 1970's is full of accounts of the towering barriers faced by parents in their efforts to get services for their children.

Robert and Suzanne Massie (1975), parents of a boy with hemophilia, wrote that they had to go to Russia to experience the comfort of people who understood their despair, and to France for an environment in which it was easier to cope with their son's hemophilia, both practically and psychologically.

Everywhere, in the schools, among doctors, I met the same reaction: Well, all right. It's very difficult, you have a hard life ... but then, c'est la vie. There is suffering in this world. People have problems. Chronic disease is one of them. No reason to stop living. *Fight*. Life is hard. Just tell us what we need to know and we'll help you if we can. (Massie & Massie, 1975, p. 341)

Whether they were right or wrong about the French, the book's account of Suzanne Massie's day-to-day struggle here in the United States to get help for Bobbie is a ringing indictment of American values, our helping professions, and our helping agencies. The Massies measured our values and found them narrow: We like health, wealth, conformity, happiness, success, competition, productivity. Given those values as ideals, what chance did disabled children have for success?

Most of us, whose disabled children are now adolescents or adults, were forced to forge our own sets of values—if family and child were to survive. Many of our children were not winners, and society reminded us of that fact everywhere we turned.

Other personal accounts document many or all of the following conditions:

1. There were acute shortages of services of all kinds—educational, vocational, recreational, social—for children with disabilities of any kind, but particularly for those with severe disabilities or combinations of disabilities.
2. There were waiting lists, with no services provided in the interim, with no time limit on the wait.
3. There were enormously high tuition or treatment fees, no tuition aid or only partial aid, or aid for only certain categories of children. Rigidly categorical programs placed the obligation upon the child to fit the program. Children with more than one disability were almost guaranteed to be ineligible everywhere, and exclusion was freely practiced.
4. Children were being referred around from one agency to another, the general rule being that the more crisis laden the child and family, the less help they got.
5. Professionals apparently thrived on "playing God," or on branding parents as rejecting or overprotective; as hostile or apathetic; as too involved or not involved enough; as having unrealistically high expectations or having none at all. It was a no-win situation for many. Pressures conspired to make them fit the stereotype of burdened parents of tragic errors, even if they felt otherwise.
6. Information about services was difficult to obtain. There were few information sources specializing in services for handicapped children. Parents stumbled upon information, learned from other parents or from a professional here or there who happened to have

made it his or her personal business to know what public or private services were available.

7. School systems and agencies could be bureaucratically unresponsive with impunity. Phone calls went unanswered, records were lost. Months were often required to collect records from various diagnosticians and schools so that an application to a new program could be completed. Records, of course, were inaccessible to parents.

8. Parents drove long distances to get their children to diagnostic or treatment "centers" or, worse still, could not get there at all.

9. The cause was not a popular one. People felt sorry for disabled children and their parents, but they didn't respect their rights. The legal profession hadn't yet noted that the handicapped were a minority victimized by exclusion and discrimination. It was hard to persuade newspapers that there was a story in it.

Newspaper exposés in the early 1970's of Rosewood and Willowbrook where retarded people were living under inhumane conditions shocked the public. Those scenes reminded them of the facts: that dreary, understaffed, overcrowded state institutions were the places to which retarded people were consigned. We had put so little value on retarded people that back wards became possible. We allowed such places to exist.

That outrage still threatens parents of severely handicapped children. It is what Greenfield's tortured account of his search for a "Place for Noah" (1978) is all about—tortured because he could not bear to define his son as does the society that still offers Noah remodeled back wards as the best available alternative to family living.

So where we "put" our children counts, and how we and others value them stems partly at least from the quality of the "places."

It takes time and effort to change attitudes. More than a decade after the exposés we still have Willowbrook, Rosewood, Partlow, and Belchertown, and we still hear of physicians who advise parents of newborn babies with Down's syndrome to put them away in such institutions, "for the sake of the family." And we continue to be plagued by neighborhood resistance to group homes for retarded people.

Disabled children growing up in the 1980's have a great advantage over their parents: They are living in a decade when it is a little more "okay" to be different.

But perhaps the events of the last two decades have had their effect on parents, too. The civil rights movement raised both personal and collective consciousness of prejudice, bias, scapegoating, discrimination, and minority rights. Litigation made it clear that the "separate but equal" doctrine was unconstitutional. I remember that in 1967, when Beckie was about six years old, listening to a Black acquaintance describe how it had felt to be excluded from restaurants, restrooms, and schools—what rage he felt. I recall being surprised to find myself identifying with much that he said. By then, Beckie had been excluded from classes for children with physical disabilities because she was retarded and excluded from classes for children who were retarded because she could not walk, and I had been repeatedly advised to put her in an institution. I was not yet feeling any inclination to fight for her rights; I did not know she had any. What I felt was the pervasive rejection, the fact that she fit nowhere in the children's world I knew of family doctors, preschools, kindergartens, and playgrounds. Unable to walk at six, she looked large and awkward in her stroller, and people stared. It was another five years before the concept of equal rights and unequal needs entered my consciousness. As a parent, I was powerfully motivated to hear it. The general public, without personal cause, may not have heard it yet.

When lawyers began to fight for the right to education for even the most severely impaired children, parents of children with substantial handicaps welcomed the special schools and classes. Typically, it may not have mattered to them whether the special education which was offered was good or bad; they were glad to have anything. When I read back over my daughter's earliest school reports, I wonder at my indiscriminate gratitude. She was not getting good special education or training as we know it now, but getting something was decidely better than nothing.

Parents of children with milder handicaps who were already in special classes came in two varieties: those who were glad to have a refuge for their children from the experience of failing in the regular classrooms, and those who were convinced that the watered-down curriculum offered in special classes was what was keeping or making their children retarded. Many of those parents were gutsy enough to fight the system on behalf of their kids, but it was a hard and unpopular struggle that generally earned the parents a reputation among school people of being trouble-makers.

Considering the formidable odds against them, they should probably be labeled heroes. Too few, though, had the nerve or know-how to engage the system in battle.

### A New Posture for Facing Problems

The interest of the legal profession, early class action suits, early legislation in some states, and, finally, federal laws have given parents some of the tools they need to advocate for their children. Today, we parents know about rights; we know about class action suits and due process; we know we can probably interest a lawyer in a case that hints of biased testing or placement, exclusion, or decisions without due process. We can also interest reporters in such happenings. And if we can't do things ourselves, there are organizations and advocacy groups to help us. Consequently, we can approach the system with a different posture. We can expect services to be provided, not as a charity but as a right. No longer threatened with exclusion, we are free to be critical, to look for quality, to demand that our children learn.

Most of us see more promise in Public Law 94-142 than we should, however. The law does nothing to assure us that special education will be plentiful or excellent, or that our children will thrive on their teachers' teaching. But it gives us tools for monitoring (the individualized education program or IEP) and for protesting decisions (due process). The changes have brought a new list of complaints from parents, and some are all too familiar:

1. *Insufficient resources and funding.* The fact that the child's special education need is stated in his or her IEP is small comfort to the parent if it cannot be met, and some services are no more available now than they were 10 years ago. For how many years must we document the same unmet needs?

2. *Teachers who are uninformed, unwilling, and, as such, unable to deal with handicapped children.* The law says inservice training for teachers and supportive staff shall take place, but more is needed.

3. *Hastily inadequately developed IEP's.* Few teachers or parents have been taught what a well-formulated IEP should include. Too many are skimpy in information, vague in goals, and prepared without input from parents, who sign them as they have been in the habit of doing, because they are required to do so.

4. *Waiting lists.* Making them illegal has not done away with them. Parents complain that psychological services, in particular, are backed up, with long waits for testing and evaluation.

5. *Placement decisions that violate common sense.* Private special educators, in some cases, are educating children better and for less cost than the public schools can. That fact is being largely ignored in many states. Parents whose children are doing very well where they are but who must be bumped on to a less restrictive environment (a private school closer to home or a public school program) are understandably distressed.

6. *Difficult-to-obtain "related services."* Just what agency or person will or will not deliver them, or will or will not pay appears to be disputed among public agencies. Transportation is mandated, but with too few buses children in our state are known to spend as long as three hours a day going to and from school. Or, when a school bus can't do the job, mainstreaming a child in a wheelchair has meant

that the child and parent deal with a succession of cab drivers who may have no wish to lift either the child or the chair. Mothers of physically handicapped children complain that the mainstream is full of back problems.

7. *Difficulties of delivering special assistance to a disabled child who is mainstreamed.* Often teachers have had no experience or training in special techniques for addressing special needs. For instance, finding someone in a regular school willing to help a child with spina bifida perform the Crede procedure is a major problem. Amassing the resources where the child is—resources of the kind or quantity that some children need—is harder than it sounds. In short, it still takes an exceptionally determined parent to see to it that needed services are delivered. The child whose parent can't or doesn't use the tools he or she has to fight with still goes without. ·

### The New Generation of Parents

As a professional, one of my jobs in the late 70's was to supervise an infant stimulation program for babies with developmental delays. I was fascinated as the year progressed by the heightened demands made by the young parents on the teachers, and by the teachers on the parents. Mutual expectations kept mounting. Toward the end of the year there was an increasingly professional give-and-take. This is not to say that the parents were free from cycling and recycling the grief that comes with having a child with a disability, but they seemed secure in the knowledge that their children had value and deserved first-rate care and education. And they, as parents, had come to feel competent to give it alongside the teachers.

What seemed to generate pain for them were encounters *outside* the program with grandparents, friends, neighbors, or others who were awkward, rejecting, or too openly sorrowful. *Within* the special program they received the support of people in the same boat. It will probably always be true that parents will at certain times need the support of fellow parents in special programs and special places, if only to fortify themselves to deal with the mainstream which may never be as hospitable to disabled people as we would wish it to be. Fortunately, the new generation of parents seems to understand that the role they must play in dealing with the general public includes an obligation to change what attitudes they can. They understand that encounters with the public, occasionally disagreeable as they may be, are risks which have to be taken. We cannot change attitudes by keeping our children out of sight.

But it is no easy job. Parents differ in their sensitivity to how others view them and their children. To some degree, we feel that *we* are defined by the way our children are treated. When we parents of disabled children see parents of normal children hurry them away from ours, we feel that we as well as our children have been judged and diminished. We can acknowledge the feeling as irrational and unwarranted; intellectually we know enough to blame the victimizer rather than our children or ourselves; nevertheless, the experience is emotionally wearing.

Recently, a fellow parent asked if I knew of any written guidelines on what to do when taking a child out in public, "say, to a restaurant." What he wanted was a list of behaviors for himself that would guarantee the acceptance by other diners of his child's presence in the restaurant and their approval of his decision to bring the child. Of course, there is no such guarantee. It helps if we like our kids and look as if we do. The important thing is to have them with us—visible as we go about our daily affairs.

Most of the new generation of parents are determinedly mainstreaming their children into the ordinary pattern of their daily activities. Most are determined proponents of the least restrictive environment in educational placements, too. I suspect, however, that if we lined up the parents of severely disabled adolescents and adults and took a vote, most would suggest that progress was all right for a while, but it went on too long. Those of us in the older generation, for the most part, *believe* as we were taught, that special schools mean skilled teachers using the best techniques and materials to give disabled children the help they need and many of us have had our belief more of less confirmed by experience. So we may not move ahead attitudinally as quickly as the law and its interpreters would like us to. Even parents and children with mild disabilities will lose patience now and then with the educators who preach normalization and integration into the mainstream of community life but ignore the gap between theory and the very real scarcity of resources that are needed to make the theory work.

The skepticism is healthy and merited, I think. Meanwhile, we all need to keep certain ideas clear in our minds:

1. In the long run, mainstreaming serves everyone's best interests. One does not bring a minority population to the public's attention or plant its needs firmly in the public's consciousness by isolating its members in special facilities. There is a difference between the strategies that knock down attitudinal barriers and those that im- ,prove special education.
2. Public Law 94-142 does not guarantee excellence in special edu-

cation. It does not even intend to address the issue of quality. What it does is insist that parents be informed about assessment and placement decisions before they happen; and it offers due process in case of disagreement. Becoming an actual part of the *decision-making process* requires that parents ask to participate and work cooperatively with school personnel to arrive at good decisions.

3. Public Law 94-142 gives parents the individualized education program (IEP). If we can develop a cooperative working relationship with teachers, principals, and specialists, the IEP gives us the opportunity to affect the substance and quality of our child's education. We can make it a point to study our child's records before the IEP conference and do some thinking. We can formulate in our own minds what goals are essential and then question closely the strategies for reaching the goals and objectives. An IEP can fail in either of two directions: by being so vague in its statement of goals that it could apply to anyone's child or so limited that it targets only a small portion of a child's needs.

4. Before signing consent, we should read the IEP carefully and sign it only if we are fully satisfied that the goals described are realistic and important, that the strategies for meeting them suit the child, that specific persons are named to be accountable for working toward the goals and objectives, and that the time framework is reasonable.

5. We should make sure that the services specified are good and that they are delivered to the child effectively. When we have the plan in hand and know the goals, the strategies to reach them, the teaching materials that should be used, who is accountable for the various activities, and when they should be taking place, we should be in a better position than ever before to monitor the *quality* of our children's education.

6. If a child is in a regular school, we must do whatever we can to make certain that the school has information about handicapped children easily available. We can ask principals to be aggressive in pursuing the means for inservice training for teachers and all supportive staff members, including the transportation staff. We can ask principals to invite parents to participate and to give teachers and other personnel the parent perspective on living with children with disabilities. Some of the most successful attitude changing has occurred in training sessions devoted to honest, open dialogues between parents and teachers.

7. Three great gaps still loom large for a disabled child who becomes an adult. One is social life. We can make sure that the schools address recreational and social needs, too. Learning leisure time

skills, how to have fun with friends, how to get around to meet people and relate to them comfortably are vital skills. Too many handicapped adults are lonely and bored.

Another is the absence of job or vocational opportunities. We can make sure that vocational education is part of the IEP early enough. We should tie into vocational rehabilitation services as soon as possible and aim for as much self-sufficiency as possible.

There is a serious shortage of supervised living arrangements for people who cannot live independently. We need to turn activist now. It is not part of the normalization plan for children to live with parents on and on into old age. Most states are lagging far behind the need and they need consistent prodding.

8. We can stay in touch with parent organizations or other advocacy groups for assistance with problems in obtaining the educational or related services our children need.

9. We can keep informed by reading and by talking with teachers, other professionals, and other parents. We can maintain a professional attitude toward parenting. We can sharpen our skills as we would to advance in any other job. We can expect no less respect from professionals than we give them.

Above all, we can keep in mind that two things are effective attitude changers: high quality of services and high visibility of children. One is of very little good without the other.

### References

Biklen, D. *Let our children go: An organization manual for advocate parents.* Syracuse NY: Human Policy Press, 1974.

Biklen, D. *The elementary school administrator's practical guide to mainstreaming.* Syracuse, NY: Human Policy Press, 1977.

Buck, P. S. *The child who never grew.* New York: John Day, 1950.

Cameron, C. C. *A different drum.* Englewood Cliffs NJ: Prentice-Hall, 1973.

Clarke, L. *Can't read, can't write, can't talk too good either: How to recognize and overcome dyslexia in your child.* New York: Walker, 1973.

Cohen, S. *Special people.* Englewood Cliffs NJ: Prentice-Hall, 1977.

Dickerson, M. U. *Our four boys: Foster parenting retarded teenagers.* Syracuse NY: Syracuse University Press, 1978.

Evans D. *Angel unaware.* Westwood NJ: Revell, 1953.

Gilhool, T. K., & Stutman, E. A. *Integration of severely handicapped students: Toward criteria for implementing and enforcing the integration imperative of P.L. 94-142 and Section 504.* Unpublished paper, 1978. Available from Public Interest Law Center of Philadelphia (Pennsylvania).

Goffman, E. *Stigma: Notes on the management of spoiled identity.* Englewood Cliffs NJ: Prentice-Hall, 1963.

Gorham (Morton), K. A., Des Jardins, C., Page, R., Pettis, E., & Scheiber, B. The effects on parents of the labeling of their children. In N. Hobbs (Ed.), *Issues in the classification of children.* San Francisco: Jossey-Bass, 1975.

Greenfeld, J. *A place for Noah.* New York: Holt, Rinehart, & Winston, 1978.

Hannam, C. *Parents and mentally handicapped children.* Baltimore: Penguin, 1975.

Hewitt, S. *The family and the handicapped child: A study of cerebral palsied children and their homes.* Chicago: Aldine, 1970.

Higgins, J. C. *Lindy.* Valley Forge PA: Judson, 1970.

Jones, R. *The acorn people.* Nashville: Abingdon, 1976.

Killelea, M. *Karen.* Englewood Cliffs, NJ: Prentice-Hall, 1952.

Kittrie, N. N. *The right to be different: Deviance and enforced therapy.* Baltimore: Johns Hopkins University Press, 1971.

Long, K. *Johnny's such a bright boy, what a shame he's retarded: In support of mainstreaming in public schools.* Boston: Houghton Mifflin, 1977.

Massie, R., & Massie, S. *Journey.* New York: Knopf, 1975.

Morton, K. A., & Hull, K. *Parents and the mainstream.* In R. L. Jones (Ed.), *Mainstreaming and the minority child.* Reston VA: Council for Exceptional Children, 1976.

Murray, D. *This is Stevie's story.* Nashville: Abingdon, 1956.

Park, C. C. *You're not alone.* Boston: Little, Brown, 1976.

Pieper, E. *Sticks and stones.* Syracuse NY: Human Policy Press, 1978.

Psy-Ed Corp. *The exceptional parent.* Author, 1972–78.

Splaver, S. *Your handicap: Don't let it handicap you.* New York: Julian Messner, 1977.

Stigen, G. K. *Heartaches and handicaps: An irreverent survival manual for parents.* Palo Alto: Science and Behavior Books, 1976.

Troisky, C. V. The hostage parent: A life-style or a challenge? *Journal of Autism and Childhood Schizophrenia,* 1978, *8* (2), 234–240.

Turnbull, A. P., & Turnbull, H. R., III (Eds.). *Parents speak out: Views from the other side of the two-way mirror.* Columbus OH: Charles E. Merrill, 1977.

Wechsler, J. *In a darkness.* New York: Ace, 1972.

# Bibliography

Readers who wish to further explore the area of attitudes toward disabled individuals should find the following bibliography most helpful. These documents were selected by searching the ERIC and Exceptional Child Education Resources (ECER) data bases. The bibliography is arranged by disability for easy reference. Documents with ED numbers may be purchased in paper copy or microfiche from the ERIC Document Reproduction Service (EDRS), P.O. Box 190, Arlington VA 22210, phone (703) 841-1212. Documents carrying the notation ED N.A. must be obtained directly from the publisher or in many cases may be ordered from The Article Copy Service—CIJE, University Microfilm International, 300 North Zeeb Road, Ann Arbor MI 48106, phone (800) 521-0600.

## Behavior Disordered

EC 11 2833                         ED N. A.
Publ. Date Nov78                        7p.
Noland, Melody;
Gruber, Joseph J.
**Self-Perception, Personality, and Behavior in Emotionally Disturbed Children.**
*Behavioral Disorders;* V4 N1 P6-12 Nov 1978

The relationship among self perception, personality, and behavior variables in 61 emotionally disturbed children (6 to 13 years old) was investigated using both univariate and multivariate data processing techniques. The reliability and objectivity of a behavior rating scale (Walker Problems Behavior Identification Checklist) were also assessed. Some of the results were that self esteem was positively related to the introversion vs. Extroversion factor and negatively related to the low vs. high anxiety factor; student assessments of their own personalities were not highly related to the teachers' ratings of behavior; and personality and behavior as rated by the teacher were significantly correlated. (Author/BD)

EC 12 2112                         ED N.A.
Publ. Date Oct 79                       5p.
Bloom, Robert B.; And Others
**The Piers-Harris Self-Concept Scale: Norms for Behaviorally Disordered Children.**
*Psychology in the Schools;* v16 n4 p483-7 Oct 1979

The Piers-Harris Self-Concept Scale was administered to 270 behaviorally disordered children (6 to 12 years old) referred to a child study center for antisocial, aggressive, and criminal behavior. Compared to the aggregate mean for published scores of normal children, Ss' scores were significantly lower and more variable. No sex, race, or age effects were observed. A table of norms for behaviorally disordered children was generated. (Author)

EC 12 4022                         ED N.A.
Publ. Date Mar 80                       6p.
Lazerson, David B.
**"I Must Be Good if I Can Teach!"–Peer Tutoring with Aggressive and Withdrawn Children.**
*Journal of Learning Disabilities;* v13 n3 p152-57 Mar 1980

The study involving 60 withdrawn and aggressive elementary school students tested the hypothesis that Ss would benefit from participating in daily learning sessions with peers having similar behavioral problems. Ss were randomly placed into three groups: tutors, tutees, and controls. After 5 weeks of peer tutoring, almost all Ss who actively participated in the program showed higher gains than control Ss in self concepts and behavioral improvement. They also showed a renewed interest in school. A significant correlation was found between gain scores and frequency of participation in peer tutoring. (Author/CL)

EC 13 0026                    ED N.A.
Publ. Date Spr 80                10p.
Lund, N. L.
Salary, H. M.
**Measured Self-Concept in Adjudicated Juvenile Offenders.**
*Adolescence;* v15 n57 p65-74 Spr 1980

The pattern of self concept scores on the Tennessee Self-Concept Scale (TSCS) was compared for a group of adjudicated juvenile offenders (N=43) and a group of nonoffenders (N=40) all 14 to 18 years old. Notable differences were obtained, which suggested areas of further research and potential areas of counseling focus in dealing with the juvenile offender. Comparisons with data provided in the TSCS Manual revealed comparable differences between the juvenile offender group and a normative group and notable similarities in score pattern between the juvenile offenders and a group of psychiatric patients. (Author)

EC 14 1887                    ED N.A.
Publ. Date 81                   143p.
Gibson, Peter McKenney
**The Effects of, and the Correlates of Success in, a Wilderness Therapy Program for Problem Youth.**

Available from UMI, P.O. Box 1346, Ann Arbor, MI 48106 ($24.00 pc, $13.00 mf) Order No. 8113511.
Columbia University.

It was concluded from a study of 89 behavior problem youths that the wilderness program was effective in bringing about changes in self concept and interpersonal competence and that these changes are not limited by S background or personal characteristics. (PHR)

## Hearing Impaired

EC 11 0315                    ED 15 4568
Publ. Date Mar78                 27p.
Garrison, Wayne M.
**Self-Concept and Social Interaction in a Deaf Population.**
EDRS mf;hc
Paper Presented at the American Educational Research Association Annual Meeting (Toronto, Ontario, Canada, March, 1978).

Investigated were self concept levels of 109 deaf college students, and examined were social interaction behaviors among a subset of 27 Ss from the study sample. Results of the Tennessee Self Concept Scale indicated a response pattern demonstrating psychological distress or maladjustment, but reliability and comprehension analysis suggested that a deaf person may approach such a test with restricted or unusual interpretations of item stimuli. Results of the performance of 27 Ss on the Social Performance Indicator revealed that assertiveness and self identity in groups were directly related to individual self concept. (CL)

EC 11 0672                    ED N. A.
Publ. Date Jun78                  4p.
Sarfaty, Linda;
Katz, Shlomo
**The Self-Concept and Adjustment Patterns of Hearing-Impaired Pupils in Different School Settings.**
*American Annals of the Deaf*; V123 N4 P438-441 Jun 1978

The impact of three different educational settings (group and individual integration and special school placement) on the self concept and adjustment patterns of 48 eighth and ninth grade hearing impaired Israeli pupils was investigated. Analysis of scores on the Tennessee Self-Concept Scale partially supported the hypothesis that Ss in integrative settings would have different self concepts and adjustment patterns than Ss in a special school. Ss in integrative settings did have higher self concepts scores, but there were no differences in the adjustment profiles among the three groups. (CL)

EC 11 2690 ED N. A.
Publ. Date Dec78 8p.
Garrison, Wayne M. and Others
**An Assessment of Self-Concept Levels Among Postsecondary Deaf Adolescents.**
*American Annals of the Deaf;* V123 N8 P968-975 Dec 1978

Self concept levels were studied in 109 post postsecondary deaf adolescents using the Tennessee Self Concept Scale (TSCS). Results indicated that Ss had lower levels of self esteem than did a normative hearing sample; however, stability analyses indicated a low reliability on this measure. Moreover, high reading comprehension among deaf Ss was found to be associated with higher self concept. Subsequent interviews with 30 of the Ss revealed that many had interpreted test stimuli peculiarly. It was concluded that the low levels of self esteem indicated by TSCS scores reflected limited understanding of the test items in their written form. (Author/DLS)

EC 11 3871 ED N. A.
Publ. Date Dec78 10p.
Garrison, Wayne M.;
Tesch, Stephanie
**Self-Concept and Deafness: A Review of Research Literature.**
*Volta Review;* V80 N7 P457-466 Dec 1978

The paper reviews some of the research literature relating to self concept and deafness, especially: (a) the types of questions posed by researchers; (b) the theoretical orientations that have guided investigations; and (c) the kinds of methodological problems that have characterized research in this field. It is noted that the severest limitation in research with deaf persons often rests with the inappropriateness of testing devices. Moreover, the need to investigate self concept from a developmental perspective is viewed as central to the task of better understanding the life adjustment of deaf individuals. (Author/PHR)

EC 14 0617 ED APR RIE
Publ. Date Apr 78 60p.
Garrison, Wayne M.; And Others
**Deafness and Self-Disclosure: Some Prob-**
**lems in Interpreting Self-Concept Measures. Paper Series No. 24.**
National Technical Inst. for the Deaf, Rochester, N.Y. Dept. of Research and Development.
Department of Health, Education, and Welfare, Washington, D.C.

The Tennessee Self Concept Scale (TSCS) was administered to 109 students newly enrolled at the National Technical Institute for the Deaf. Consistent with earlier reserch literature, test results indicated that the deaf students had lower levels of self esteem than did the normative hearing population. Subsequent interviews with 30 members of the study sample revealed, however, that many of the deaf students had interpreted the test stimuli peculiarly, thus affecting their scores on the TSCS in a negative manner. It was suggested that questionnaire type measures of affective variables (or psychological well being) which fail to take into consideration the linguistic and experiential deficits of the deaf respondent may create false impressions of psychological maladjustment. A sample copy of the TSCS is appended. (Author/SB)

EC 14 0619 ED APR RIE
Publ. Date [78] 23p.
Garrison, Wayne M.
Tesch, Stephanie
**Self-Concept and Deafness: A Review of Research Literature. Paper Series No. 27.**
National Technical Inst. for the Deaf, Rochester, N.Y. Dept. of Research and Development.
Department of Health, Education, and Welfare, Washington, D.C.
EDRS mf;hc
For related documents, see EC 140 611-630.

The paper reviews some of the research literature relating to self concept and deafness. In summarizing the relevant research, attention was given to the types of questions to which researchers have sought answers, the theoretical orientations which have guided investigations, and the kinds of methodological problems which have characterized research in this field. It was noted that the severest limitation in research with the deaf rested with the inappropriateness of testing devices, a situation not uncommon to research on personality attributes of other groups of persons. Moreover, the need to investigate self concept from a developmental perspective was viewed as central to the task of better understanding the life adjustment of the deaf individual. (Author)

EC 14 0677      ED MAY RIE
Publ. Date Mar 81      29p.
Convey, John J.
Koelle, William H.
**Improving the Prediction of Achievement of Deaf Adolescents by Modifying a Locus of Control and a Self-Concept Instrument.**
EDRS mf;hc
Paper presented at the Annual Meeting of the Eastern Educational Reseach Association (Philadelphia, PA, March 12-14, 1981).

Each item of the Rotter Locus of Control Scale and 28 of the 80 items of the Piers-Harris Children's Self Concept Scale wre revised because of syntax or vocabulary that were considered to be problematic for deaf adolescents. The original and modified forms of each instrument were administered to 90 deaf adolescents from four residential schools. Better prediction was obtained for six of the nine subscales of the Stanford Achievement Test for the Hearing Impaired when scores from the modified forms of the instruments were used as predictors in place of scores from the original forms of the instruments. Other predictors were parent hearing status, sex, age, and school. Generally, parent hearing status and self concept were the most important predictors of the achievement subscales; however, the increase in prediction that occurred when the modified forms of the instruments were used as predictors was due particularly to the locus of control variable. Tables with statistical data are appended. (Author)

# Learning Disabled

EC 11 0351      ED 15 3402
Publ. Date May78      14p.
Myers, L. Kay Hartwell;
Wiseman, Douglas E.
**Attitudes of the Adolescent Learning Disabled Students Related to School Relationships, Teacher Relationships and Learning.**
EDRS mf;hc
Paper Presented at the Annual International Convention, the Council for Exceptional Children (56th, Kansas City, Missouri, May 2-5, 1978, Session T47).

Examined were the self concept and attitudes of 88 learning disabled (LD) adolescents related to school, teacher, family relationships, and specific learning disabilities. Ss were administered a 59-item questionnaire. Among findings were that LD students indicated positive experiences and attitudes of peers, regular and special classroom teachers, and family; and LD students did not perceive many of the negative social relationships discussed in the literature or the negative personal, behavioral, and learning characteristics attributed to them by the few studies in this area. (SBH)

EC 11 0637      ED N. A.
Publ. Date Jul78      7p.
Sheare, Joseph B.
**The Impact of Resource Programs upon the Self-Concept and Peer Acceptance of Learning Disabled Children.**
*Psychology in the Schools*; V15 N3 P406–412 Jul 1978

Measured was the impact of resource interventions on peer acceptance and self concept of 41 learning disabled elementary students. Analysis of scores from the Piers-Harris Self Concept Scale and the Peer Acceptance Rating Scale indicated that Ss were significantly lower in both ratings compared to a nonlearning disabled control group. The resource program did not result in significant changes in either self concept or peer acceptance after 1 year. (CL)

EC 11 0790      ED N. A.
Publ. Date May78      5p.
Ribner, Sol
**The Effects of Special Class Placement on the Self-Concept of Exceptional Children.**
*Journal of Learning Disabilities*; V11 N5 P319–323 May 1978

The self concept of 386 minimally brain damaged children (8 to 16 years) in special classes was compared with that of 96 children with similar disabilities who were in regular classes. Analysis of questionnaires on school adequacy and general competency revealed that Ss in regular classes had significantly lower self concepts in school adequacy but not in general competence. When compared with normal Ss, both groups of brain damaged Ss had significantly lower self concepts in school adequacy, but only Ss in regular classes held significantly lower self concepts than normal Ss in general competence. No relationship was found between self concept and length of stay in special classes. (Author/CL)

EC 11 4661    ED 169 738
Publ. Date Apr79    24p.
Chapman, James W.;
Boersma, Frederic J.
**Self-Perceptions of Ability, Expectations and Locus of Control in Elementary Learning Disabled Children.**
EDRS mf;hc
Paper Presented at the Annual Meeting of the American Educational Research Association (San Francisco, April, 1979, Session 16.05).

Affective development was investigated in 81 learning disabled (LD) and 81 normal achieving (control) children in grades 3 through 6. The Students' Perception of Ability Scale and the Projected Academic Performance Scale were used to assess academic self concept and future achievement expectations. Academic locus of control was tapped by the Intellectual Achievement Responsibility Questionnaire. Strong differences were observed between the LD and control Ss on these three affective variables. The history of school failure that typifies LD students appeared to be associated with more negative self perceptions of ability, external attributions of responsibility for school successes, and lower expectations of future success in academic tasks. (Author/SBH)

EC 11 4742    ED N. A.
Publ. Date Apr79    6p.
Chapman, James W.;
Boersma, Frederic J.
**Academic Self-Concept in Elementary Learning Disabled Children: A Study with the Student's Perception of Ability Scale.**
*Psychology in the Schools;* V16 N2 P201-6 Apr79

Academic self concept as measured by the Student's Perception of Ability Scale (SPAS) was compared for 81 learning disabled (LD) and 81 normally achieving control children in grades 3 to 6. Results

showed that LD children hold significantly more negative self perceptions of ability in reading, spelling, and arithmetic than do the control children. Further, the negative school subject-related attitudes in the LD children had generalized to lower self perceptions of ability in general, to expressions of less confidence in school, and more negative attitudes toward school. No grade level or sex effects were observed. It was concluded that the SPAS is able to discriminate between normally achieving children and those experiencing problems in school. (Author/SBH)

EC 11 5130    ED N. A.
Publ. Date May79    5p.
Stewart, Donald J. and Others
**Response Instability on the Piers-Harris Children's Self-Concept Scale.**
*Journal of Learning Disabilities;* V12 N5 P351-5 May79

The study involving 60 Ss investigated whether response instability differs significantly among self concept levels of elementary and junior high learning disabled (LD) students, whether elementary and junior high LD students differ significantly on item response instability, and whether response instability is significantly related to age, sex, race, or IQ. Ss were administered the Piers-Harris Children's Self-Concept Scale. Among findings was that LD students at both elementary and junior high levels demonstrate considerable item instability when reporting self concept. (SBH)

EC 11 5211    ED 171 002
Publ. Date Apr79    25p.
Kendall, William S.
**The Learning Disabled Adolescent: An Overview of Affective Education and Career Development Practices.**
EDRS mf;hc
Paper Presented at the Annual International Convention, the Council for Exceptional Children (57th, Dallas, Texas, April 22-27, 1979, Session B-5)

Thirty learning disabled (LD) students enrolled in secondary regular classes, 30 LD Ss in vocational training classes, and 30 LD Ss integrated in regular secondary classes and receiving additional assistance in learning resource centers were compared on measures of self concept and career attitudes. Results from the attitude scale of the Career Maturity index and the Illinois Index of Self Derogation were analyzed, and significant differences were found among the means of the self concept and career attitude scores of the three groups. Self concepts of LD Ss in vocational training and learning resource centers were lower than that of regular class Ss. The learning resource group demonstrated lower career attitude scores than the vocational training and regular class Ss. Findings supported vocational training classes as the most efficacious in shaping career attitudes of LD adolescents. (CL)

EC 12 2972                          ED N.A.
Publ. Date Dec 79                        6p.
Smith, Monte D.
**Prediction of Self-Concept Among Learning Disabled Children.**
*Journal of Learning Disabilities;* v12 n10 p664-69 Dec 1979

The investigation explored the possibility of predicting self concept among 147 learning disabled children (ages 7 to 13) on the bases of several combinations of predictor variables. Verbal IQ, performance IQ, and reading performance variables had little relationship to self concept. The combinations of word knowledge performance, math performance, and family socioeconomic status (SES) significantly predicted self concept. Somewhat surprisingly, learning disabled children from high SES families had lower self concepts than their low SES counterparts. (Author/PHR)

EC 12 3697                          ED N.A.
Publ. Date 79                            8p.
Cohn, Linda
**Social Isolation in the School Pictures of Learning-Disabled Children: A Research Study.**
*Art Psychotherapy;* v6 n4 p277-84 1979

The study examined the interpersonal relationships and manifest social isolation of learning disabled (LD) children by comparing the drawings done by 15 LD children and 16 normal children (all between the ages of 6 and 16). Results demonstrated that the LD children depicted themselves as socially iso-

lated in the context of their school environment. A grotesque self image and the omission of peers from the drawings appeared significantly more in the drawings of LD children than in those of normal children. (DB)

EC 12 2511                          ED N.A.
Publ. Date Win 79                       10p.
Boersma, Frederic J.; And Others
**Academic Self-Concept Change in Special Education Students: Some Suggestions for Interpreting Self-Concept Scores.**
*Journal of Special Education;* v13 n4 p433-42 Win 1979

Changes in academic self concept, as measured by the Student's Perception of Ability Scale, were studied in 50 learning disabled, 18 educable mentally retarded elementary special education students receiving full time remedial placement and 83 regular class students. The results of pre-post data collected over a 12 month period revealed that full time placement was accompanied by statistically significant increases in academic self concept, especially in the areas of reading/spelling and confidence. The discussion deals with possible causes for these changes, e.g., achievement gains and peer reference group comparisons. Implications of the findings in terms of assessing changes in academic self concept as a function of remedial placement are discussed. (Author)

EC 12 2657                          ED N.A.
Publ. Date Fal 79                        4p.
Bryan, Tanis
Pearl, Ruth
**Self Concepts and Locus of Control of Learning Disabled Children.**
*Journal of Clinical Child Psychology;* v8 n3 p223-6 Fal 1979

Studies of the self concept and locus of control of learning disabled children indicate that learning disabled children are more likely than nondisabled children to have negative self concepts, to believe that their successes are the result of luck or other people; and that their failures are insurmountable. It has been found that these maladaptive attitudes and attributions are established by about nine years and become increasingly more negative with age. In addition, parents and teachers hold more negative expectations for the future achievements of learning disabled children than of nondisabled children; their expectations are even more negative than the learning disabled hold for themselves. Intervention programs should include teaching the learning disabled to cope with failure. (Author/PHR)

EC 13 0256          ED N.A.
Publ. Date Sum 80          6p.
Yauman, Beth E.
**Special Education Placement and the Self-Concepts of Elementary-School Age Children.**
*Learning Disability Quarterly;* v3 n3 p30-35 Sum 1980

The study investigated the relationship between degree or extent of special education participation and measured self concept with 45 third grade male students divided into three groups (students in self contained LD classes, students provided individual tutoring, and a control group of students from regular classes). The results indicated a significant difference among the three groups on both reading achievement and self concept measures. With the effect of reading achievement covaried out, no significant difference remained among the three groups on measured self concept. Rank ordering and statistical pairwise comparison of self concept scores indicated poorer self concepts for the tutored group despite higher achievement levels than the self contained group. (Author/PHR)

EC 13 0373          ED N.A.
Publ. Date Sep 80          18p.
Thomson, Michael E.
Hartley, Gill M.
**Self-Concept in Dyslexic Children.**

Available from UMI
*Academic Therapy;* v16 n1 p19-36 Sep 1980

The self esteem of 15 eight to ten year old children with dyslexia was compared to a matched control group of normal or above average readers. Relationships were examined among the following six constructs: good at reading, kind, hard working, intelligent, happy, and successful. Among findings were that the dyslexic children did not associate ability at reading and intelligence with kindness to the extent that the control group did and that dyslexic children felt inadequate

in both the school and home environment. (PHR)

EC 13 1771          ED 197 564
Publ. Date 80          13p.
Johnson, Charlotte F.
**The Arkansas Committee for LD Adults: Another Dimension.**
EDRS mf;hc

Available from ACLD, Inc., 4156 Library Rd., Pittsburgh, PA ($2.00).
Paper presented at the Annual Meeting of the Association for Children with Learning Disabilities (17th, 1980).

A four part survey involving 30 learning disabled (LD) adults was undertaken to investigate Ss' attitudes toward being LD, toward best sources of help, toward cause of disability, and thinking styles. Among findings were that help from other LD people was considered the best source of help, that half the group attributed the LD problem to a physical brain injury, that responses supported a hereditary predisposition as a possible causative agent of both stress and brain functioning problems, and that a common extreme cognitive style exists. (SBH)

EC 13 2052          ED N.A.
Publ. Date Fal 80          8p.
Chandler, Theodore A.
**Reversal Peer Tutoring Effects on Powerlessness in Adolescents.**
*Adolescence;* v15 n59 p715-22 Fal 1980

Thirteen seventh and eighth graders with high external locus of control, low academic achievement, and negative attitudes toward school and/or self were trained as tutors for other students like themselves. Significant changes were noted toward internality on the Bailer Children's Locus of Control Scale. Teachers reported progress in subject matter performance and positive attitude changes for 81% of the Ss. (CL)

EC 14 0302          ED APR RIE
Publ. Date Jan 81          21p.
Arnoni, Gila; And Others
**Self and Ideal Self of Learning Disabled Children–A Preliminary Study.**
EDRS mf;hc
Paper presented at the Annual Meeting of the Southwest Educational Research Association

(Dallas, TX, January, 1981). Print is light in parts and may not reproduce well.

Ten learning disabled (LD) and 10 nonLD 10 to 11 year old children were administered the Bledsoe Self Concept Scale twice: first they were asked to respond in terms of how they perceive themselves and second, as how they would like to be. Contrary to hypotheses, results indicated that LD and nonLD Ss did not differ significantly in self concept or in congruence between self and ideal self concepts. (A 12 page review of the literature on self concept preceeds the account of the study.) (CL)

EC 14 0703        ED N.A.
Publ. Date Nov 81        9p.
Morrison, Gale M.
**Perspectives of Social Status of Learning-Handicapped and Nonhandicapped Students.**

Available from UMI

*American Journal of Mental Deficiency;* v86 n3 p243-51 Nov 1981

The social status of 40 mildly learning handicapped and 24 nonhandicapped students and their own perceptions of and their ideal preference for social status were investigated. In Study 1 the social status perspectives of handicapped vs. nonhandicapped students in a regular class environment into which the mildly learning handicapped students had been mainstreamed was compared. Results indicated that the mildly handicapped children overestimated their social status in the direction of their ideal. In Study 2 the social status perspectives of the same mildly learning handicapped students in two classroom settings were compared. Although these children overestimated their social status in the regular class setting, their estimates and ideals were accurate in their special class settings. Implications for intervention were discussed. (Author)

EC 14 1137        ED JUL RIE
Publ. Date Aug 81        16p.
Murphy, Beverly Fuller
**A Study of Self-Concept Improvement in Learning Disabled Children as Measured by a Modified Burk's Rating Scale.**
Evansville Univ., Ind.
EDRS mf;hc

To examine self concept development in learning disabled (LD) children, a behavior rating scale was given to parents and teachers of 27 LD students (6 to 15 years old) in a summer program which provided activities to enhance the self concept. Parents' and teachers' perceptions of the children's self concept changed signficantly as a result of the program; however, only the parents' scores increased in a positive direction. (A list of the self concept activities used in the program is appended.) (CL)

EC 14 1937        ED N.A.
Publ. Date 81        83p.
Jordan, Guy Winford
**Performance of Learning Disabled and Average Achieving Pupils on Selected Self-Concept Measures.**

Available from UMI, P.O. Box 1346, Ann Arbor, MI 48106 ($24.00 pc, $13.00 mf) Order No. 8116881.
University of Georgia.

Findings of a comparison study of 40 learning disabled and 40 normal achieving fourth and fifth grade students showed that there is a significant difference in self concept between the learning disabled and normal achiever. Analysis indicated that teacher ratings of self concept on the behavior rating form was the primary contributor to that difference. (PHR)

## Mentally Retarded

EC 11 0491        ED N. A.
Publ. Date Apr78        3p.
White, William F. and Others
**Self-Concept Correlates in Academic Placement of Secondary School Students.**
*Perceptual and Motor Skills;* V46 N2 P360-362 Apr 1978

Forty-three eighth graders assigned to vocational education courses on the basis of low standardized test scores in reading and math were administered a self concept inventory, the Me Scale. The hypothesis that Ss would have lower and more negative self concept feelings than students not assigned to basic education classes (n 91) was not supported. Lower achieving Ss perceived themselves as more capable in manual dexterity than higher achieving Ss. (CL)

EC 11 2926          ED N. A.
Publ. Date Win78          4p.
Calhoun, George, Jr. and Others
**An Investigation of the Goode-nough-Harris Drawing Test and the (Coopersmith) Self-Esteem Inventory.**
*Educational and Psychological Measurement;* V38 N4 P1229-1232 Win78

The relationship between scores on a self drawing test and a self perception test was assessed with 16 primary and secondary grade educable mentally retarded students (ages 6 to 12 years). Among the findings was a significant correlation between scores on the Goode-nough-Harris Drawing Test and scores on the Self-Esteem Inventory for the secondary Ss but not for the primary Ss. (Author/DLS)

EC 11 4918          ED N. A.
Publ. Date Spr79          9p.
Cohen, Libby
**The Influences and Effects of Labeling on the MR by Their Peers.**
*Journal for Special Educators;* V15 N3 P204-12 Spr79

A review of research on labeling persons mentally retarded focuses on the role of perceived subnormality, IQ differences, negative behavior, and special class placement on peer acceptance and self concept. It is emphasized that social skills instruction and approaches to decreasing negative behavior should be emphasized. (CL)

EC 11 5223          ED 171 014
Publ. Date Apr79          19p.
Prieto, Alfonso G.;
McCoy, Kathleen
**Perceived Roles and Educable Mentally Handicapped Minority Students.**
EDRS mf;hc
Paper Presented at the Annual International Convention, the Council for Exceptional Children (57th, Dallas, Texas, April 22-27, 1979, Session T-20)

The study involving 16 male Mexican American students and 16 Anglo students (10 to 12 years old) who had been categorized as educable mentally handicapped (EMH) was conducted to examine the relationship between special education labels and race, and student and teacher perception on scores of the Modified Bem Sex-Role Inventory (BSRI). The teacher was first asked to rate a student on his/her perception of the student, and students were then asked to rate themselves. Findings were summarized into the following points: (1) teachers' perceptions of normal students are very similar regardless of race; (2) EMH students are perceived differently from normal students by teachers, and teachers also differ in their perceptions of Chicano EMH and Anglo EMH students; (3) normal Chicano students and normal Anglo students share common perceptions of themselves; and (4) Anglo EMH students perceive themselves to be very much like the normal students. The Chicano EMH students, however, perceive themselves very differently than do normal Anglo, normal Chicano, and EMH Anglo students. (Graphs showing statistical data are included.) (SBH)

EC 12 0645          ED N.A.
Publ. Date Jul 79          5p.
Simpson, H. M.
Meaney, Cheryl
**Effects of Learning to Ski on the Self-Concept of Mentally Retarded Children.**
*American Journal of Mental Deficiency;* v84 n1 p25-29 Jul 1979

Changes in the self concept of 14 trainable mentally retarded children as a function of experience in a ski program were evaluated. A control group received similar pre- and postmeasures of self concept but did not participate in the ski program. Significant changes in self concept occurred among students in the experimental but not the control group. Furthermore, the magnitude of success in learning to ski was shown to be positively and significantly correlated with magnitude of change in self concept. (Author/CL)

EC 12 0773          ED 177 755
Publ. Date May 78          87p.
Litrownik, Alan J.
**Self-Concept and Self-Regulatory Practices in TMRs. Final Report.**
San Diego State Univ., Calif. Dept. of Psychology.
Bureau of Education for the Handicapped (DHEW/OE), Washington, D.C.
EDRS mf;hc
Print is marginally legible on some pages.

The purpose of the project was to develop and evaluate a training program in self regulatory skills with approximately 40 trainable mentally retarded students (TMR) (mean age 18 years) and to determine the effect of the acquired self regulatory skills on task performance and self concept. In Phase 1, six preliminary studies attempted to determine (1) whether TMR students could perform these requisite skills, (2) if these skills could be developed in students who did not have them, and (3) the effects of these acquired skills on task performance. Results indicated that few TMR students had appropriate self regulatory skills, but that these skills could be acquired, generalized, and retained as a result of a brief training period. The second phase involved evaluation of a training program with features appropriate to other structured (e.g., classroom) situations. Two groups were trained in the component self regulatory skills of self monitoring, self evaluation, and self reward, with one group having appropriate external standards of performance set and the other allowed to set its own standards of performance. Two additional groups served as controls. Results indicated (1) that trained students reached criterion and independently transferred self regulatory skills to new tasks; (2) that trained students, especially those who set their own appropriate standards, outperformed other groups; and (3) that there were no differences in self concept between the trained and control groups. (PHR)

EC 12 1638          ED N.A.
Publ. Date Jun 79          4p.
Semmel, Melvyn I.
Cheney, Christine O.
**Social Acceptance and Self-Concept of Handicapped Pupils in Mainstream Environments.**
*Education Unlimited;* v1 n2 p65-68 Jun 1979

The paper reviews selected research findings relative to the social acceptance/rejection and self concept of handicapped students in regular classroom environments. Studies are limited to those involving educable mentally retarded, learning disabled, or behaviorally disordered children. It is concluded that mildly handicapped pupils were rejected by their normal peers prior to the advent of mainstreaming and that there is evidence that this social rejection continues to be a serious impediment to their growth. (SBH)

EC 12 3946          ED N.A.
Publ. Date Mar 80          5p.
Parish, Thomas S.; And Others
**Normal and Exceptional Children's Attitudes Toward Themselves and One Another.**
*Journal of Psychology;* v104 n2 p249-53 Mar 1980

A study investigated the attitudes of 65 normal and disabled junior high students toward themselves and one another. It was found that Ss evaluated themselves most favorably, normal children as a group less favorably, and exceptional children as a group least favorably of all on the Personal Attribute Inventory for Children. This was so regardless of whether the respondents were normal or exceptional children. Since data were collected from mainstreamed classrooms, it appears that mainstreaming may not be directly deleterious to exceptional children's self concepts, but has associated with it a negative stigma for exceptional children as a group, for both exceptional and normal children. These findings, plus others reported previously, fail to demonstrate that mainstreaming in its present form may be an elixir for exceptional children's social-emotional difficulties. (Author/DLS)

EC 12 4965          ED N.A.
Publ. Date Jul 80          6p.
Reiter, Shunit
Levi, A. M.
**Factors Affecting Social Integration of Noninstitutionalized Mentally Retarded Adults.**
*American Journal of Mental Deficiency;* v85 n1 p25-30 Jul 1980

A group of 30 moderately and mildly retarded young adults (study group) was compared with a group of borderline retarded (control group) adults on employability, behavior at work, social integration and social skills, personality, and self concept. Findings indicated that the study group was less well integrated at work and in society than was the control group and showed lack of social skills. The retarded adults who had nonretarded friends showed better social/educational skills than did the other Ss. (Author/PHR)

EC 13 1325          ED 196 198
Publ. Date 80          12p.

Luftig, Richard L.
**The Effect of Differential Educational Placements on the Self Concept of Retarded Pupils: A Review.**
EDRS mf;hc
Paper presented at the Annual Meeting of the American Educational Research Association (1980).

The paper analyzes research on the self concept of differentially placed educable mentally retarded (EMR) students and hypothesizes covarying factors which may suggest to educators variables to be taken into account in placement decisions. Considered are such factors as IQ, reading achievement, and being the only retarded child mainstreamed into a class. Among conclusions are that high IQ EMR students seem to do well in a mainstreamed environment in terms of self concept while low IQ EMR student maintain significantly higher self concept in mainstreamed classes whereas children with poorer reading skills maintain higher self concept in self contained classes; and that to place a child in an educational environment in which he cannot maintain feelings of self worth may actually increase rather than decrease the restrictiveness of the school environment. (SBH)

EC 13 2833                    ED OCT RIF
Publ. Date [78]                        23p.
Roswal, Glenn
Frith, Greg H.
**The Effects of Physical Activity on Self Concept, Risk-Taking Behaviors, and Motor Functioning in Mildly Handicapped Individuals: A Literature Review.**
Jacksonville State Univ., Ala.
EDRS mf;hc

Literature is reviewed regarding the impact of physical activity on development in mildly handicapped (educable mentally retarded and learning disabled) students. Studies showing improvement in self concept after participation in a motor development program are cited. Risk taking in the mildly retarded is examined, and the implications of a change toward optimal risk taking behavior are thought to involve improved self concept and peer relations. Findings of relationships between motor proficiency and improved physical fitness as well as intellectual devel-

opment are pointed out. The authors conclude that a structured activity program should have significant implications for the development of mildly handicapped children. (CL)

EC 13 2881                    ED NOV RIE
Publ. Date 80                          12p.
Uno, Tad
Leonardson, Gary
**Creativity and Self Concept of Mentally Retarded Adolescents.**
EDRS mf;hc

The relationship between self concept and creativity was examined in 44 mentally retarded adolescents. Self concept was measured by the Piers-Harris Children's Self Concept Scale. Physical health and quality of home life were rated. Creativity measures included the Alternate Uses Test and Torrance's Thinking Creatively with Pictures, Form B. Results indicated a self concept score slightly below the normative mean and a significant correlation with perceived health scores. Self concept and intelligence were not significantly correlated, nor, contrary to the hypothesis, were self concept and creativity. In fact, the Torrance nonverbal measures were negatively, but not significantly correlated with self concept. Significant negative correlations were found between creativity and perceived physical health and home life. Results were taken to support the contention that a single measure of creativity is insufficient. (CL)

EC 13 3316                    ED 203 631
Publ. Date [79]                        28p.
Chassin, Laurie; And Others
**Self-labeling by EMR High School Students in Their Mainstream and Special Education Classes.**
Arizona State Univ., Tempe.
EDRS mf;hc

Available from Laurie Chassin, Department of Psychology, Arizona State University, Tempe, AZ 85281.

Fifty-nine educable mentally retarded (EMR) students and 330 nonhandicapped high school students from mainstream classes completed semantic differential ratings of a stereotypic Popular Teenager, Juvenile Delinquent, and Special Education Student. Ss also rated their global self concepts and situation specific self concepts within the mainstream and the special class settings. Ratings were done at the beginning (Time 1) and the end (Time 2) of a semester. Results showed that mainstream classes did not delabel EMR students. Within the mainstream class, the number of EMR students who saw themselves as similar to a special education student significantly increased over time. Moreover, at Time 2, EMR students were more likely to think of themselves as similar to a special education student in their mainstream class than in their special education class. Howver, EMR students' global self concepts did not change. (Author/SB)

EC 13 3473                     ED N.A.
Publ. Date Fal 80                    6p.
Wheeler, Larry
Reilly, Thomas F.
**Self-Concept and Its Relationship to Academic Achievement for EMR Adolescents.**

Available from UMI
*Journal for Special Educators;* v17 n1 p78-83 Fall 1980

The relationship between self concept and academic achievement was examined with 30 educable mentally retarded adolescent residents of a state institution. Ss were given the "How I See Myself Scale" and the "Peabody Individual Achievement Test." Results failed to demonstrate a positive relationship between self concept and academic achievement in the areas of mathematics and reading. (DB)

EC 14 1622                     ED N.A.
Publ. Date Jan 82                    8p.
Leahy, Robert L.; And Others
**Role-Taking, Self-Image, and Imitativeness of Mentally Retarded and Nonretarded Individuals.**

Available from UMI
*American Journal of Mental Deficiency;* v86 n4 p372-79 Jan 1982

Retarded (N=24) and nonretarded (N=46) individuals matched on MA and CA were tested on role taking, self image, and imitation. Higher IQ, MA, real self image, and ideal self image were associated with less imitation. Higher IQ and MA were related to more positive ideal self image, and higher

MA was related to more positive real self image. Retarded individuals had less positive real and ideal self images compared to the nonretarded groups but were equal to the MA matched nonretarded group on role taking ability. The findings supported the view that role taking ability is a function of cognitive level and that self image and imitation are determined by both cognitive and experiential factors. (Author)

## Physically Disabled/ Other Health Impairments

EC 11 1774                     ED 15 7289
Publ. Date Jun78                    10p.
Bishop, Elizabeth S.
**Self-Concept and Family Relations in Physically Handicapped Adolescents in British Day and Residential Special Schools.**
EDRS mf;hc
Paper Presented at the World Congress on Future Special Education (First, Stirling, Scotland, June 25 - June 30, 1978).

A number of social, home adjustment, and self concept measures were administered to 200 physically handicapped adolescents in British special schools. No significant differences were found in terms of self concept, family relations, social adjustment, or attitudes toward the disabled between the 100 day school Ss and the 100 residential school Ss. Likewise, no differences were seen when comparisons were made between those with acquired and congenital handicaps or those with more or less severe handicaps. Males did have more positive self concepts than females. (Author/SBH)

EC 13 0488                     ED N.A.
Publ. Date Dec 79                    3p.
VanPutte, Alison W.
**Relationship of School Setting to Self Concept in Physically Disabled Children.**
*Journal of School Health;* v49 n10 p576-78 Dec 1979

Identifiers: *Spina Bifida;

The relationship between school setting (mainstreamed or sheltered) and self concept in 20 students (ages 7 to 15) was investigated. Results showed essentially no relationship between the two, however, a statistically significant correlation was found which associated both older age and higher socioeconomic status with lower self concept scores. (Author/PHR)

EC 13 2623                          ED N.A.
Publ. Date Dec 80                        8p.
Landon, Christopher; And Others
**Self-Image of Adolescents with Cystic Fibrosis.**
*Journal of Youth and Adolescence;* v9 n6 p521-28 Dec 1980

A self image questionnaire was administered to two groups of cystic fibrosis (CF) adolescents (16 males and 8 females) and one group of 34 otherwise healthy males with short stature and/or delayed puberty. CF males showed an abnormal pattern of adjustment that could be considered comparable to disturbed males and growth delayed and sexually delayed males. The CF female group was concordant with the normal population. The fact that CF and pubertally delayed males have a self perception of maladjustment to the psychologic problems of adolescence suggests that adjustment problems of the CF male may be related to growth retardation and pubertal delay. The social stigma of which may be more easily disguised in the female. (Author)

EC 14 1989                          ED N.A.
Publ. Date 81                          97p.
Lesh, Kay Christensen
**The Effects of Support Services on the Self Concept, Locus of Control and Goal Attainment of Physically Disabled College Students.**

Available from UMI, P.O. Box 1346, Ann Arbor, MI 48106 ($24.00 pc, $13.00 mf) Order No. 8117739.
The University of Arizona.

From the study, involving 21 physically disabled college students, it was concluded that neither adaptive physical education nor group counseling have a statistically significant effect on the self concept or locus of control of the physically disabled Ss. (SB)

## Visually Impaired

EC 12 1981                          ED N.A.
Publ. Date Sum 79                        5p.
Head, Daniel N.
**A Comparison of Self-Concept Scores for Visually Impaired Adolescents in Several Class Settings.**

Available from UMI
*Education of the Visually Handicapped;* v11 n2 p51-55 Sum 1979

Self concept scores from 62 blind and low vision adolescents were compared across the predominant class placements for the visually impaired (residential, resource room, itinerant). Although no statistically significant results were obtained, it was noted that the itinerantly served Ss exhibited the lowest self concept scores. Data also revealed similar self concept scores for blind and low vision Ss. (Author/CL)

EC 12 2732                          ED N.A.
Publ. Date Fal 79                        8p.
Coker, Gary
**A Comparison of Self-Concepts and Academic Achievement of Visually Handicapped Children Enrolled in a Regular School and in a Residential School.**

Available from UMI
*Education of the Visually Handicapped;* v11 n3 p67-74 Fall 1979

The academic achievement and self concept of 20 visually handicapped children (grades 3 through 6) in regular day schools were compared to visually handicapped students in grades 3 through 6 in residential schools. The data indicated that achievement scores for students enrolled in residential schools were higher for the fourth, fifth, and sixth grade levels than those of students enrolled in regular day schools. Both groups had overall positive self concepts with individual significant differences between the groups in the areas of intellectual and social status and physical appearance and attributes. (Author/PHR)

EC 13 1627                          ED N.A.
Publ. Date Nov 80                        5p.
Lambert, Robert
West, Malcolm

**Parenting Styles and the Depressive Syndrome in Congenitally Blind Individuals.**

Available from UMI
*Journal of Visual Impairment and Blindness;*
v74 n9 p333-37 Nov 1980

The article discusses the effect on congenitally blind children of three types of parents: those who are overprotective, those who push the child toward independence too soon, and those who are "good enough." The authors focus on how the three styles of parenting affect the blind child's ability to give and receive and develop a sense of competence. These effects are discussed in the context of the ego ideal. The authors also examine the depressive core that is often the result of the blind child's inability to live up to the dictates of the ego ideal. Finally, they suggest a fourth style of parenting that would prepare blind children better for the problems they will encounter in the sighted world. (Author)

EC 13 1934                    ED N.A.
Publ. Date Fal 80                9p.
Head, Daniel N.
**The Stability of Self-Concept Scores in Visually Impaired Adolescents.**

Available from UMI
*Education of the Visually Handicapped;* v12 n3 p66-74 Fall 1980

The stability of self concept from junior high to senior high school was examined for 62 blind and low vision adolescents in residential, resource room, and itinerant class placements. While no significant differences for this group were determined as a function of grade level or visual loss, a significant interaction effect between these variables did occur. A further analysis showed a significant increase in self concept scores for the low vision Ss as a function of grade level placement. (Author)

EC 13 3445                    ED N.A.
Publ. Date Jun 81                6p.
Cook-Clampert, Denise
**The Development of Self-Concept in Blind Children.**

Available from UMI
*Journal of Visual Impairment and Blindness;*
v75 n6 p233-38 Jun 1981

Research (both data based and descriptive) on the development of self concept in sighted and blind children is reviewed. Unanswered questions regarding family's childrearing methods, anxiety level, and the growth of positive self concept are cited. The educator's role in promoting the blind child's self esteem is emphasized. (CL)